THINGS TO DO IN
RETIREMENT
THAT UNLEASH PLAY, PASSION, AND PURPOSE

A SIMPLIFIED GUIDE TO FUN AND MEANINGFUL ACTIVITIES REGARDLESS OF FINANCIAL, PHYSICAL, OR SOCIAL LIMITATIONS

KD CARR

THINGS TO DO IN RETIREMENT THAT UNLEASH PLAY, PASSION, AND PURPOSE

A SIMPLIFIED GUIDE TO FUN AND MEANINGFUL ACTIVITIES REGARDLESS OF FINANCIAL, PHYSICAL, OR SOCIAL LIMITATIONS

KD CARR

"And in the end, it's not the years in your life that count. It's the life in your years."

— ABRAHAM LINCOLN

CONTENTS

INTRODUCTION

So here you are, on the threshold of a new chapter in life, buzzing with anticipation yet possibly feeling somewhat overwhelmed. That's precisely where I stood at the onset of retirement. The relentless pace of work deadlines, meetings, and family commitments faded away, leaving a vast expanse of time ready to be filled. The initial silence, a stark contrast to the daily hustle of work and family life, initially felt odd. However, as I embarked on this new journey, I uncovered passions and opportunities that were once hidden from me. This book is born from that exploration—an immersion into a retirement life brimming with happiness, creativity, and many surprises.

At its heart, this book is committed to showing you that an extraordinary retirement is within reach for everyone, no matter your budget, physical abilities, or social circles. It's about inspiring you to seek out those activities that light up your eyes and heart. It's about crafting the retirement you've always envisioned but perhaps never thought possible.

This book, structured in easy-to-navigate sections, walks you through many activities—from the simple joys of gardening to the thrill of digital adventures. Each chapter has practical advice, uplifting stories, and direct links to resources supporting your new endeavors. We'll cover the essentials of adapting to this significant life change, tackling common concerns such as identity shifts and health worries with optimism and practical strategies.

Why focus on play, passion, and purpose? Retirement isn't just an extended vacation. It's a time for a renaissance—a period to reinvent yourself, connect deeply with others, and contribute meaningfully to your community. Through engaging anecdotes and evidence from those who've turned their golden years into their most vibrant yet, this book illustrates how integrating these elements can significantly enrich your life.

Retirement can seem daunting. You might worry about becoming irrelevant or running out of things to do. That's why I've included stories of real people who found renewed purpose and joy in this chapter of their lives. These narratives are not just motivational; they show the diverse ways retirement can be a fulfilling, dynamic time.

This book is for everyone. Whether you're an outdoor enthusiast, an aspiring artist, or a novice curious about tech, there's something here for you. And speaking of technology, don't worry—I've made sure to explain it in a way that's clear and accessible, helping you to connect with the broader world and maybe even master a new skill or two.

So, consider this your invitation to join me on this adventure. Retirement is a journey best enjoyed with curiosity and a readiness to explore. By the end of this book, you'll have a tailor-made list of activities to dive into, each promising to enrich your days.

Let's shake off any apprehensions and step confidently into this exciting phase. Let's discover how you can make your retirement both relaxing and genuinely remarkable. Welcome to your vibrant, engaging, and fulfilling retirement—it starts right here, right now. Let's get started, shall we?

TRANSITIONING INTO RETIREMENT WITH EASE

W ho said life after labor is just lounging and lemonade? Not us, that's for sure. If you're picturing your post-work years as an endless loop of daytime TV and searching for your glasses (only to find them perched on your head), think again. Retirement is the secret backstage pass to the rock concert of life —and you've just been handed yours. This chapter is about turning the volume up on your retirement years and dancing to the beat of newfound freedom and possibilities.

Let's kick things off by addressing the elephant in the room—or the fear lurking in the corner. It's not uncommon to feel like a ship unmoored when you first retire. Where do you sail to when the structured harbors of 9-to-5 life are behind you? Well, it's time to navigate these waters with the enthusiasm of an intrepid explorer. First, let's get that retirement mindset tuned to the right frequency.

CULTIVATING A POSITIVE RETIREMENT MINDSET

Retirement isn't the final act; it's an intermission followed by a spectacular second show. Don't think of it as closing a door but as opening several others—each leading to exciting new adventures. This phase is your opportunity to rediscover old passions you've shelved, learn new skills, or even start that business idea that's been simmering on the back burner for decades.

But here's a little secret: The transition can be as smooth as your favorite jazz tune if you adjust your mindset to see this as a beginning rather than an end. It's about tuning into a new frequency where the possibilities are endless. You've got the time now, and how you use it can turn retirement into one of the most fulfilling times of your life.

Now, let's talk fear because it's the first thing that wants to crash our retirement party. Losing a sense of identity or purpose tops the list of retirement fears. After all, many of us have spent most of our lives tied to job titles and careers that dictate who we are. But here's the twist: retirement allows you to redefine yourself on your terms.

It's normal to feel adrift, but anchor yourself with this thought: you are not your job. You are the ship's captain and can steer it wherever you want. Begin by listing things you always wanted to do but couldn't do while working full-time. Whether painting, writing, woodworking, rekindling long-lost friendships, or even scuba diving, now's the time to explore these avenues. Each step into something new rebuilds your identity around your passions, not your past profession.

If retirement were a weather forecast, it would be an eternal spring—an ideal time for growth and renewal. This stage of life can be as vibrant and exciting as you make it. Shift your outlook by focusing on the freedom ahead.

You now have the liberty to choose how each day unfolds. Want to start the morning with a walk instead of a commute? Go for it. Are you interested in learning Spanish or picking up pottery? Sign up for that class. By viewing retirement as a blank canvas you get to paint every day, you'll find that it's not just about filling time but making time fulfilling.

Uncertainty can be thrilling. It's the spice of life that keeps things interesting. Retirement throws many unknowns your way, but each unknown is a hidden gem waiting to be discovered. Instead of dreading the uncertainty, embrace it as an adventure.

Try this: Do something completely new once a month. It could be visiting a town you've never been to, starting a blog, or volunteering in a field outside your wheelhouse. These ventures into the unknown can lead to unexpected joys and discoveries you wouldn't encounter otherwise. Embracing uncertainty turns every day into a treasure hunt where you're both the mapmaker and the explorer.

So, as we navigate the mists of retirement, remember this: the waters may be uncharted, but they are yours to explore. With each new day, you can chart a new course as unique and vibrant as a coral reef teeming with life. Let's set sail toward a retirement filled with purpose, passion, and plenty of play.

SETTING GOALS FOR YOUR NEXT CHAPTER

Imagine retirement as an expansive garden. When you first step into it, everything seems possible—every corner is an opportunity to plant new seeds for flowers you've never grown. But just as in gardening, a flourishing retirement needs a bit of planning. You wouldn't just scatter seeds willy-nilly and hope for the best, right? Similarly, defining a clear vision of what you want your retirement to look like is the first crucial step toward cultivating a life that truly satisfies and excites you.

Start by asking yourself what a fulfilling retirement looks like for you. It's not just about filling time; it's about filling life with the things that stir your soul. Did you always want to write a book? Learn to paint? Travel to the vineyards of France or the temples of Thailand? You may want to spend more time with family, start a small business, RV across the country, or become a volunteer. Retirement is your time. Sketch a vision that includes all the hobbies, dreams, and aspirations you shelved during your working years. Imagine your ideal week in retirement—what activities are you engaging in, who are you with, and how do you feel? This vision acts as your North Star, guiding your decisions and aligning you with your true desires.

Creating a Vision Board for Your Retirement

Creating a vision board is a fantastic way to visualize and plan your future. Here's a step-by-step guide to help you develop your retirement vision board:

1. Gather the Necessary Materials:

- A large board or poster (corkboard, foam board, or poster board)

- Magazines, newspapers, printouts, or any other sources of images and text
- Scissors
- Glue, tape, or push pins
- Markers, pens, or pencils
- Decorative items (stickers, washi tape, etc.)

2. Define Your Vision: Think about what retirement means to you. What are your goals, dreams, and desires for this stage of life? Topics to consider include (but are not limited to) travel, hobbies, family time, health, and personal growth.

3. Gather Images and Words: Look through magazines, newspapers, or online sources for images, words, and phrases that resonate with your vision of retirement. Cut out anything that inspires you or represents your goals. Don't overthink while doing this. Go with your gut instinct.

4. Sort Your Materials: Organize your cutouts into categories, such as travel, hobbies, family, health, lifestyle, etc. This process will help you create a more structured vision board.

5. Plan Your Layout: Arrange your materials on the board before gluing or pinning anything down. Play around with the layout until it feels right. Ensure that the most critical elements are prominent and highly visible.

6. Create a Focal Point: Choose a central image or word embodying the essence of your retirement vision. Place it in the center of the board to serve as the focal point.

7. Add Your Images and Words: Start gluing, taping, or pinning your images and words to the board. Work from the center outward, ensuring everything is securely attached.

8. Personalize Your Board: Use markers, pens, or pencils to add notes, dates, or specific goals. You can also add decorative items like stickers, washi tape, or other embellishments to make your vision board uniquely yours.

9. Reflect and Adjust: Take a step back and view your vision board. Does it represent your retirement dreams and goals? If not, make any adjustments as needed.

10. Display Your Vision Board: Place your completed vision board where you will see it regularly. Seeing it daily will remind you of your retirement aspirations and motivate you.

11. Review and Update: Review your vision board periodically to ensure it aligns with your goals. As your vision evolves, update your board with new images and ideas.

Creating a vision board is a personal and creative process, so there's no right or wrong way to do it. Have fun, and let your imagination guide you! Getting together with friends and having a vision board party is also great fun. Everyone brings their magazines, inspiration, laughs, and materials to share.

Here is an example of what a vision board might look like for someone who wants to travel, connect with old friends and family, pursue new hobbies, and stay active to maintain health:

Now, with your vision clearly defined, it's time to set some concrete, achievable goals. Defining your goals isn't about setting lofty targets that leave you feeling deflated if you don't reach them —it's about setting realistic ones that motivate you. Break your vision down into manageable goals. If you want to write that book, start with, "I will write for an hour three days a week," rather than, "I will have a bestseller in a year." It's about progress, not perfection. Remember, the beauty of retirement is that you control your deadlines. Your goals should inspire you, not pressure you.

Flexibility is your friend here. While it's great to have goals, it's also essential to stay open to new interests and opportunities that might come your way. You may start a cooking class and discover a passion for Italian cuisine or join a hiking club and find that you love birdwatching. Life is wonderfully unpredictable, and your interests might evolve as you explore the vast landscape of retirement. Allow yourself the flexibility to adjust your goals as you grow. Think of your plan more as a compass than a map; it should guide you but not constrain you.

Creating a timeline can help you turn these dreams into reality. Think about what you would like to achieve in the short term (next three months), medium term (next year), and long term (next five years). Create milestones that build on each other, bringing you closer to your vision. For instance, if traveling is part of your dream, short-term goals might include researching destinations or saving a certain amount each month. Medium-term goals could be to make reservations and prepare an itinerary; a long-term goal might be to embark on a three-month tour of Europe.

Setting goals for your retirement is about continuing to grow, explore, and enjoy life, with each day bringing something to look forward to. By clearly defining your vision, setting achievable goals, embracing flexibility, and mapping out a timeline, you're not just planning for a fruitful retirement—you're setting the stage for a spectacular new chapter just waiting to be written.

NAVIGATING CHANGES IN DAILY ROUTINES

Ah, retirement! It's like finally turning off the alarm clock after decades of the same jarring morning ritual. At first, it feels fantastic—endless days stretching before you, no meetings, no deadlines. But then, the novelty wears off, and you might wonder, "What day is it anyway?" Transitioning from a structured workday to the expansive openness of retirement can be like stepping into a wide-open prairie after years in a bustling city—it's beautiful but a bit disorienting.

Adjusting to this new rhythm doesn't have to be an arduous task. It starts with acknowledging that while you don't have to punch a clock, creating some structure can prevent those "what do I do now?" moments. Begin by sketching out a loose daily schedule. Perhaps mornings are for exercise, afternoons are for hobbies, and evenings are for socializing or relaxing. The beauty here is in the flexibility—you're the boss now, and if you want to switch things up, you absolutely can.

Creating a new routine involves finding a balance between freedom and structure. Start by incorporating activities that bring you joy and adding new ones you've always wanted to try. If you're a morning person, consider starting your day with a cup of coffee while watching the sunrise. Craft your days to begin with something you love, setting a positive tone for the rest of the day. After breakfast, dedicate time to a hobby like gardening, painting, or writing when your energy is at its peak. Utilize post-lunch hours for a leisurely walk with a friend or listen to an engaging podcast. Evenings are ideal for joining a community class, having dinner with friends, or enjoying a good book. The key is to fill your day with activities that nourish your body, mind, and soul, keeping you active, engaged, and connected.

Now, let's talk rituals because here's where the magic happens. Rituals are those small, repeated actions that give our days texture and meaning. They can be as simple as a morning stretch, an afternoon tea break, or journaling before bed. These aren't just tasks on a checklist; they're touchstones that bring a comforting rhythm to your days. They anchor you, remind you of what's most important, and introduce a steady cadence to the newfound freedom of your days. Maybe it's the ritual of reading the newspaper each morning or calling an old friend every Sunday. These actions become the scaffolding around which you build your day, providing just enough structure to keep you grounded.

Staying active and engaged turns the golden years into truly golden experiences. It's not just about keeping busy but about engaging deeply in life. Physical activity is a cornerstone here, whether it's yoga, swimming, or daily walks through your neighborhood. But let's expand our definition of activity to include mental and social engagement. Learn a new skill, join a book club, volunteer, or even start a blog. Remember, keeping your brain sharp is as important as moving your body. Social connections, too, play a crucial role in our well-being, especially during retirement. These interactions keep us laughing, thinking, and feeling connected to the world around us.

By thoughtfully crafting your days with a mix of personal rituals, structured activities, and ample room for spontaneity, you create a retirement lifestyle that's as vibrant and fulfilling as any working year—perhaps even more so. After all, isn't the freedom to live our days as we choose the ultimate luxury? And you've earned it, so go ahead and fill your days with the richness they deserve.

FINANCIAL PLANNING FOR FUN, NOT JUST NECESSITIES

Welcome to the wild and wonderful world of retirement finance, where every penny saved is a ticket to adventure, and budgeting doesn't mean skimping on the fun. Think of this chapter as your trusty financial GPS, guiding you through the scenic route of savings and spending without leading you off a fiscal cliff. It's all about balancing the art of frugality with the joy of splurging because, let's face it, counting pennies should never mean counting out your dreams.

CREATIVE BUDGETING FOR YOUR DREAM ACTIVITIES

Retirement might mean the end of your paycheck, but it's just the beginning of mastering the art of stretching your dollar. First things first: Let's do a financial health check-up. Start by reviewing your savings, pension, and any other income sources. Are they pulsing with vitality, or do they need a bit of CPR? Understanding where you stand financially gives you the clarity to make decisions that won't leave your wallet gasping for air.

Let's carve that financial pie into enough slices to satisfy your needs and wants. Bills and groceries are nonnegotiable, but your hobbies and leisure activities should still get the crumbs. Allocate funds for fun—that's right, make joy a line item in your budget. Determine how much you can comfortably spend on leisure each month without dipping into the essentials. Plan to set aside a specific percentage of your income for entertainment, travel, and hobbies. Remember, a budget that includes pleasure is sustainable because all work and no play makes your retirement a very dull affair.

Now we get crafty. Let's trim down expenses in other areas to free up more funds for the fun stuff. Start with the low-hanging fruits like utility bills—consider energy-efficient appliances, or, better yet, become a coupon-clipping ninja. Maybe renegotiate your internet and cable services or switch to a less expensive provider. And let's not forget about repurposing and recycling—those old jars? Perfect for your new painting hobby. Every dollar you save is a dollar you can spend on a passion project or a new adventure.

Are you dreaming of a European escapade or a Caribbean cruise? Big dreams require big plans—and sometimes a sizeable piggy bank. Start by identifying your dream activities and estimating the costs. Once you have a target in mind, it's time to strategize. Consider setting up a dedicated savings account for this goal and making regular contributions. It could be as simple as redirecting a small portion of your monthly income or any extra windfalls— like that birthday check from Aunt Mildred—straight into this fund. And remember, patience is vital. Rome wasn't built in a day, and your dream vacation fund might take time to grow, but oh, the places you'll go when it does!

Consider maintaining a financial journal to keep your financial goals in perspective and ensure you're on track. Regular entries can help you reflect on your spending habits, reassess your budget allocations, and stay motivated. Here's a prompt to get you started: "This month, I spent money on things that made me happiest. Were these purchases planned? How do they align with my financial goals?" This practice sharpens your financial strategy and aligns your spending with joyful, fulfilling retirement goals.

MAXIMIZING RETIREE DISCOUNTS AND DEALS

Retirement isn't just about kicking back and enjoying the slow life; it's also about reaping the rewards of those years of hard work through some nifty financial perks known as senior discounts. Yes, it's time to embrace every coupon, discount, and deal that comes your way to save money and as a golden ticket to explore new experiences without straining your wallet.

When it comes to finding these fabulous discounts, the world is truly your oyster. Start with the obvious suspects: restaurants, movie theaters, and retailers. Many businesses offer discounts to seniors, usually starting at the age of 55 or 60. But here's a pro tip: Always ask, even if you don't see a discount advertised. The worst they can say is no, and you might just be surprised at how many places are willing to give you a price break. For travel deals, websites like SeniorDiscounts.com or the AARP Travel Center can offer reduced rates on hotels, flights, and even car rentals. Are you dining out? Websites like TheSeniorList.com regularly update lists of restaurants that offer discounts to seniors. Remember, a penny saved is a penny you can spend on making more retirement memories.

Now, let's talk about memberships. Joining organizations like AARP can be like finding a financial fairy godmother for seniors. For a small annual fee, AARP membership opens up a world of savings on everything from dining to insurance to vacation packages. Imagine slashing hotel bills, saving on health services, and even getting discounts on car rentals. And it's not just about the discounts; these memberships often come with added perks like free financial advice, which can be incredibly valuable when navigating the complexities of retirement finances. Think of it as an investment that keeps giving, cushioning your budget, and enhancing your lifestyle.

For the local adventurers, don't overlook the deals hidden in your own backyard. Many community centers, local theaters, museums, and even service providers offer senior discounts that could significantly lower the cost of your activities. Local newspapers or community bulletins often advertise these deals, and joining local Facebook groups or checking community boards can also lead you to some fantastic finds. Whether it's a discounted pottery class at the community center or a lower-priced ticket to a local concert, these local deals can make everyday activities more frequent and fun without breaking the bank.

But why view discounts merely as a way to save money? Each discount is a door to an experience that might have been off your radar. They are opportunities to step out of your comfort zone and try something new. That discounted ticket to a jazz concert may reveal a newfound love for live music, or a reduced entry fee to a gardening workshop might unearth a passion for horticulture. Discounts can be the nudge you need to explore, learn, and grow in unexpected ways during your retirement.

And let's not forget about the digital age, where even savings have gone tech-savvy with online cashback applications. Apps like Rakuten, Honey, and Ibotta offer cashback on purchases from both online and brick-and-mortar stores. Sign up, shop through their portals, and watch the cashback amounts accumulate. Then, there's Dosh, which automates the process by linking directly to your credit card—spend as you usually would and receive cashback without lifting a finger. And don't forget Fetch Rewards, which allows users to earn points by scanning their receipts for purchases made at various stores. My favorite is Groupon, which offers steeply discounted prices on merchandise, restaurant gift cards, and experi-

ences. Groupon is a great way to push yourself out of your comfort zone and try new things without paying high ticket prices.

In retirement, every discount, membership, and deal adds a splash of color and excitement, enabling you to paint a lifestyle rich in experiences yet considerate of your budget. So, embrace the age of discounts with open arms and a ready smile, for each penny saved is a step toward another adventure, another story, and another day well spent in the delightful retirement journey.

AFFORDABLE TRAVEL HACKS FOR THE ADVENTUROUS RETIREE

When exploring the vast and varied world of retirement, the savvy traveler knows that the art of adventure doesn't have to come with a hefty price tag. Dive into the delightful realm of off-peak travel, where the crowds thin out and the rates tumble down. Imagine having the Louvre almost to yourself or strolling through the streets of Santorini without the summer swarm. Traveling during these quieter times significantly cuts costs and enhances your experience, immersing yourself deeply in local culture without the usual hustle and bustle. Now, while you're smartly dodging the peak seasons, why not smarten up your travel game with the magic of reward programs? Airlines, hotels, and credit cards are practically throwing points at you, and who are you to say no? Sign up for these programs and watch as your everyday purchases rack up points that you can redeem for flights, hotel stays, and even car rentals. The trick is to stay loyal to a few key providers to maximize your benefits. It's like planting seeds that grow into free travel trees. Imagine jetting off to a new destination using points accumulated from last year's grocery shopping!

As you collect points, consider why you should settle for standard hotel rooms when the world offers an array of quirky and affordable accommodations. From home exchanges to short-term rentals and even cozy senior hostels, the options are as varied as they are economical. Home exchanges, for instance, allow you to swap your home with someone else's in another part of the world, offering a truly authentic and cost-effective way to live like a local. Meanwhile, platforms like Airbnb and Vrbo connect you to short-term rental opportunities that often provide more space and amenities than hotels at a fraction of the cost. And let's not overlook senior hostels, which are wallet-friendly and great places to meet fellow globetrotting retirees.

When choosing your next destination, why not venture off the beaten path? Countless budget-friendly locales offer rich cultural experiences without the lavish price tags of their more famous counterparts. Places like Portugal, Malaysia, and even certain Eastern European areas offer stunning historical sites, delicious cuisine, and warm hospitality without draining your travel fund.

These destinations allow you to stretch your dollar further to see more, do more, and stay longer.

Speaking of staying longer, let's touch on voluntourism, a unique way to extend your travels without extending your budget. Volunteering in exchange for accommodation, meals, or even travel expenses allows you to immerse yourself in new cultures, make meaningful contributions, and meet like-minded travelers while keeping costs low. Whether helping with wildlife conservation in Africa or teaching English in Southeast Asia, voluntourism provides an enriching way to see the world. We will explore this topic further in the book, but it's worth noting here for its significant cost-saving potential.

If you want to travel closer to home, RVing is an excellent way to see the country more affordably and meet new people. Many retirees love traveling, camping, and exploring in a recreational vehicle (RV). RVing encompasses a variety of experiences, from weekend camping trips to full-time living on the road. We will explore this topic more deeply later.

Through strategic planning and some creativity, the world opens up to you in retirement without breaking the bank. Embrace these affordable travel hacks to enrich your life with experiences, not expenses. Remember, the goal is to make memories that are priceless, not expensive.

As this chapter closes and we prepare to dive deeper into the enrichments of retirement, remember that each strategy, tip, and insight shared here is a stepping stone to a broader, more vibrant world of possibilities. Looking ahead, we'll continue exploring how connecting with communities, embracing new hobbies, and engaging with the world around you can enrich your retirement journey in unexpected and fulfilling ways. Let the adventures continue!

STAYING CONNECTED—SOCIAL ACTIVITIES AND NETWORKS

Retirement is when you can finally kick back, relax, and … start panicking about how much free time you have! But fear not, for the world is your oyster or, perhaps more fittingly, your social club. Gone are the days when you filled your calendar with mandatory office gatherings, and the most exciting moment was deciding between two sugars or cream. Now, it's time to fill your days with groups and clubs that spark not just conversation but genuine joy and interest. Whether you're into knitting, karate, or kite flying, there's a club waiting for you. And if you can't find one, why not start one?

JOINING CLUBS THAT MATCH YOUR INTERESTS

First, let's figure out what floats your boat or tickles your fancy. You might think you know what you like, but a hidden passion for watercolor painting or salsa dancing might be waiting to emerge. Start by listing activities you've always been interested in, no matter how outlandish they may seem. Have you always wanted to try your hand at archery? Add that to your list. Are you fascinated by birdwatching? Add that one, too. This list is your catalog of potential, and it's as unique as you are. Take your time; remember, curiosity did not kill the retiree—it made their day much more interesting.

Now that you've got your list, it's time to play matchmaker between you and your ideal club. Finding a club is like online dating but less daunting, with a higher chance of meeting like-minded souls. Start your search locally. Community centers, libraries, and even local cafés

often have bulletin boards with club advertisements. Don't forget to harness the power of the internet—sites like Meetup.com can be goldmines for finding groups that share your specific interests. Whether it's a book club that revels in murder mysteries or a hiking group that enjoys leisurely strolls rather than scaling mountains, there's something out there for everyone.

But what if you've searched high and low and can't find the club of your dreams? Well, why not start your own? Launching your own club is like throwing a party where the only people invited enjoy the same things as you. Start by deciding the group's focus, then spread the word through friends,  family, and local community boards. Social media can also be a powerful tool to attract members. Create a catchy name for your group, set up regular meeting times, and plan your first few activities. Being the founder of a club puts you at the center of the action and allows you to help steer the group's activities toward things you're passionate about.

Let's talk about the why. Why should you even bother joining or starting a club? Because the benefits of engaging in social hobbies stretch far beyond filling your calendar. These activities can significantly boost your mental and emotional well-being. Social interactions can keep your mind sharp, improve emotional resilience, and enhance physical health. Clubs provide a sense of community and belonging, which is crucial during a time in life when significant transitions are taking place. They can act as your support network, entertainment, and family. From sharing laughs over a failed pottery project to supporting each other through personal milestones, these connections can enrich your life in ways that solo activities simply cannot.

To maximize the benefits of your social activities, consider journaling about your experiences in these clubs and groups. Reflect on questions like, "What did I enjoy most about today's meeting?" or "How do I feel after participating in this activity?" This reflection not only allows you to appreciate your active social life but also helps you identify which activities are genuinely fulfilling. Adjust your involvement based on these insights, ensuring your social life is as vibrant and nurturing as possible.

During retirement, social clubs and groups are the threads that add color, texture, and strength. They turn the abstract concept of community into a beautiful quilt of faces, names, and shared experiences. Weave these threads into a lovely pattern that enhances your life by exploring your interests, connecting with like-minded individuals, and even starting your own group. Whether through laughter-filled evenings, thoughtful discussions, or the collective sigh of satisfaction at the end of a group project, these social connections forge a network of support and friendship that can make all the difference in your retirement years. So take that first step and watch as your social world expands in the most delightful ways.

VOLUNTEERING: GIVING BACK WHILE MAKING FRIENDS

When you think of retirement, you might imagine endless leisure days, but here's a twist – how about adding a sprinkle of purpose to that mix with some volunteering? It's like adding a dash of salt to your favorite dish; it enhances the flavor! Volunteering isn't just about giving back; it's a two-way street that offers as much to the giver as the receiver. Let's unpack how you can dive into volunteering, make fantastic new friends, and fill your days with rewarding experiences that light up your heart and perhaps even your Facebook feed.

Choosing the right cause to volunteer for is like picking a new show to binge-watch—you want something that grabs your interest and, ideally, touches your heart. Start with what you're passionate about. Is it education, health, the environment, or perhaps the arts? Maybe you've always had a soft spot for animals or a keen interest in history. Whatever tugs at your heartstrings is a good starting point. Now, think about what you're good at. Maybe you're a wizard with numbers, a master gardener, or have a knack for cooking. These skills are your superpowers in the volunteering world. Organizations always need skilled volunteers; using your talents to help others can be incredibly fulfilling. Local community centers, churches, and nonprofits often have volunteer coordinators to help you find a cause that matches your interests and skills. Websites like VolunteerMatch.org and Idealist.org can also connect you with organizations needing help.

Finding the proper volunteering gig is like finding the perfect coffee shop—you want somewhere you can feel at home and meet new people. Look for volunteer opportunities that allow for social interaction. Helping at a local food bank, tutoring kids, working in community gardens, or even helping at animal shelters are great

ways to give back and connect with others who share your values and interests. You may foster friendships that can add a rich community layer to your life. Remember, volunteering is flexible. You can choose how much time you commit, whether for a few hours a week or for a specific project. This flexibility is perfect for retirees who want to balance giving back with enjoying their freedom.

Now, let's talk perks. And no, not just the free coffee or the occasional donut, though those are a bonus. Volunteering provides profound rewards that can enhance your life. The joy comes from knowing you're making a difference—it's like an instant mood booster. Then there's the social aspect. Volunteering can be incredibly social, whether you're collaborating on projects, celebrating successes, or simply sharing experiences with fellow volunteers. These interactions can lead to friendships that are both meaningful and inspiring. Plus, staying active and engaged can have significant health benefits, including lowering stress and keeping your mind sharp. In many ways, volunteering is a wellness activity—one that nourishes your soul and keeps you healthy.

Volunteering abroad might be the ticket for those with a zest for adventure and a passion for cultural exchange ("Voluntourism," previously mentioned earlier in this book). Imagine teaching English in a school in Thailand, working on conservation projects in the Amazon, or helping with community development in Africa. Not only do you get to travel and see new places, but you also do so in a meaningful and impactful way. It's a way to experience the world that goes beyond the typical tourist paths, allowing you to connect with local communities and cultures on a deeper level.

This type of volunteering often requires more extensive planning and commitment, but the rewards are equally substantial. We'll dive deeper into how to make the most out of volunteering abroad later, but it's worth considering if you're looking for an adventure that feeds your soul and shows you the world through a different lens.

In retirement, volunteering is one of the threads that add color, texture, and depth. It offers a unique blend of social interaction, personal growth, and the joy of giving back, making it a fulfilling part of your post-work life. Whether you're teaching, building, planting, or just lending a hand, each act of volunteering connects you to a larger purpose and a community of like-minded individuals. It's a chance to build new friendships, explore new passions, and positively impact the world. And really, what could be more rewarding than that?

USING TECHNOLOGY TO STAY IN TOUCH AND MAKE NEW FRIENDS

This is an age where your smartphone holds more than just your contacts—it's your window to the world, your photo album, and your lifeline to keeping up with the grandkids' antics. Mastering the art of digital communication is like finding the fountain of youth. It keeps you spry, social, and in the loop. We'll demystify social media and digital communication later, ensuring you're keeping up and leading the pack in the digital fast lane.

PHYSICAL ACTIVITIES FOR EVERY ABILITY

Retirement is when you finally get to focus on the essential things in life, like discovering whether you're more of a yoga mat warrior or a park-walking enthusiast. But let's not jump into the jogging pants just yet! This chapter is all about finding that sweet spot between breaking a sweat and fostering inner peace. Think of it as your guide to staying active—regardless of the date on your birth certificate.

GENTLE YOGA SEQUENCES FOR FLEXIBILITY AND PEACE

First, let's talk yoga—no, not the pretzel-twisting, "How does she even bend that way?" kind, but the gentle, restorative yoga that's perfect for everyone. Whether you are as flexible as a rubber band or as stiff as a board, yoga is the go-to activity for maintaining flexibility, balance, and a Zen-like calm that would make a monk nod in approval. But how do you start if touching your toes feels like a distant dream? Easy! Modification is your best friend. Chairs, cushions, and even the trusty wall can transform a seemingly impossible pose into a piece of cake. For instance, if a standard yoga pose calls for you to be on the floor, using a chair for support can help you achieve the pose without the risk of turning into a human knot. The key is to listen to your body and adjust the poses to suit your comfort level—there's no competition here, just gentle progression.

Now, you might wonder, "Why yoga?" Aside from allowing you to wear those trendy yoga pants, it offers many benefits that are perfect for the golden years. For starters, yoga is excellent for enhancing flexibility, which helps keep those bothersome aches and pains at bay. But that's not all; it's also a champion at reducing stress and boosting mental clarity. Imagine starting your day not with a blaring alarm but with a peaceful yoga routine that leaves you feeling rejuvenated and ready to take on the world—or at least your garden. Yoga's meditative practices focus on breathing and mindfulness, helping clear the cobwebs from your mind and fostering a sense of peace throughout the day.

Are you thinking of trying yoga? Great! You'll need a few essentials to get started, but don't worry—you won't have to break the bank. A good yoga mat is your foundation. Look for one with enough cushioning to protect your joints and a nonslip surface to keep you steady. A couple of yoga blocks and straps can also be invaluable, especially when starting. These tools help you extend your reach and maintain poses without straining. Remember, the goal is comfort and stability, so choose equipment that makes you feel secure and supported.

In the age of the internet, the best yoga instructor might not be in a studio near you but right on your screen. Online yoga classes are a fantastic resource, especially for retirees who prefer a session in the comfort of their living room. Platforms like YouTube offer many free yoga videos, ranging from beginner-friendly sequences to more advanced sessions. Look for classes tagged as "gentle," "senior," or "restorative" to start with—they usually focus on flexibility and relaxation, perfect for easing into your yoga practice. Websites like Gaia and YogaGlo also offer tailored yoga programs for a modest subscription fee, providing structured routines and professional guidance that you can enjoy from home.

Yoga is more than just a physical practice; it's a way to align your body, mind, and spirit through gentle stretches and calming breaths. Integrating yoga into your life can be transformative, whether you're a seasoned yogi or a curious newcomer. It's about taking that step—no matter how small—toward a healthier, more peaceful you. So, roll out that mat, take a deep breath, and embrace the gentle flow of retirement yoga. Your body (and mind) will thank you.

FUN AND SAFE EXERCISES FOR CARDIOVASCULAR HEALTH

Think of your heart as the battery that powers the flashlight of your life; the more robust the battery, the brighter the beam. Maintaining a healthy cardiovascular system doesn't require you to become the next marathon champ. A mix of moderate activities can keep your heart pumping efficiently without turning you into a gym rat. Let's dive into the heart of the matter—finding fun and safe exercises that keep you feeling young at heart without overdoing it.

First, swimming is a stellar choice for those looking to improve their cardiovascular health. It's like giving your body a bear hug from the water, providing resistance that tones muscles while the buoyancy minimizes strain on joints. One of my best friends, whom I'll refer to as Jan, had long suffered from chronic back pain due to scoliosis. A few years back, she also faced a breast cancer diagnosis. After her courageous battle and recovery, Jan felt an immediate need to make the most of her time and soon retired.

Swimming had always been a cherished activity formed in her younger years, yet adulthood responsibilities had significantly limited her pool time. Upon retiring, Jan eagerly joined a local indoor pool and committed to swimming five days a week. These daily swims reignited a forgotten passion and introduced her to a community of fellow swimmers. Over time, Jan experienced remarkable improvements in her health; she shed pounds, her physique became more toned, and most importantly, her back pain became much more manageable. Today, years into this routine, Jan and her pool friends, who have grown closer, regularly engage in social activities like dining out, attending plays, and more. For Jan, returning to swimming didn't just enhance her physical health—it enriched her life in ways she never anticipated, proving that it's never too late to rediscover old passions and cultivate new friendships.

Another exercise option is cycling, either outdoors or on a stationary bike. It's perfect for a scenic spin around the park or an episode of your favorite show while pedaling. You may also be interested in exploring e-bikes, which have become increasingly popular. They are a great way to exercise and have  battery-powered pedal assist functionality, providing extra help with climbing those steep hills you might typically avoid.

Dancing also makes this list; whether it's ballroom dancing, line dancing, or a solo dance party in your living room, it's all about moving to the beat of your heart. And let's not forget about rowing, which can be done on a rowing machine inside or in the great outdoors. It's a fantastic way to work the heart and lungs while catching up with a friend in a dual rowing boat or kayak.

A balanced workout routine should include aerobic exercises, strength training, and flexibility routines. Aerobics get your heart rate up and improve cardiovascular endurance. This could be anything from brisk walking to a Zumba class. On the other hand, strength training, such as using resistance bands or light weights, helps build muscle and supports bone health, which is crucial as we age. Flexibility exercises like stretching or Pilates enhance muscle elasticity and prevent injuries. Aim to blend these elements throughout the week, switching things up to keep it exciting and fun. Remember, the goal is to enjoy the process. If it feels like a chore, it's time to reevaluate and inject some more fun into the mix.

However, discussing the exercises that might warrant a caution sign is crucial. High-impact activities, such as running on hard surfaces or high-intensity interval training (HIIT), can sometimes pose risks, especially if you have joint issues or cardiovascular concerns. It's always a good idea to consult a healthcare provider to tailor your exercise choices to your specific health needs. Additionally, exercises that involve heavy lifting or can cause abrupt changes in blood pressure, such as overhead lifts or power-lifting, should be approached with caution or avoided altogether. Safety first, as they say. There's no medal for pushing through pain unnecessarily.

Monitoring your health during exercise is not just about watching for signs of distress; it's about understanding your body's feedback loop. Keeping an eye on your heart rate can tell you if you're in the "fat burn" zone or pushing into the "danger" zone. A simple way to monitor your heart rate is to use a fitness tracker, which has models that vary in price and functionality. Many models today also offer features like heart rate alerts, which notify you when your heart rate exceeds a set limit. Additionally, pay attention to how you feel during and after exercise. Symptoms like undue fatigue, dizziness, or chest pain are red flags and should prompt you to stop and seek medical advice. Remember, the aim is to boost your health, not push it to the brink.

As we continue to explore the many ways to keep our bodies vibrant and vigorous, it's clear that a thoughtful approach to physical activity can lead to a healthier, happier you. Whether swimming laps, cycling through the countryside, or dancing your heart out, the right mix of enjoyable and safe exercises can help maintain your cardiovascular health and overall zest for life. Keep moving, keep laughing, and keep your heart in the game because every beat counts in the beautiful rhythm of retirement.

THE JOY OF WALKING CLUBS

So, you've decided to take your strolls to the next level by starting a walking club? Bravo! Imagine a group where each step boosts your health and connects you with like-minded folks who share your enthusiasm for fresh air and friendly chatter. Setting up a walking club is less about speed and more about community; it's like orchestrating a parade where everyone's invited and the pace is comfortable.

Let's walk through the steps, shall we? First, pinpoint what kind of walking club you want. Is it for brisk walkers or a more leisurely pace that allows for birdwatching and photo ops? Knowing your audience helps tailor the club to meet specific interests and fitness levels. Next, spread the word. Use community bulletin boards, social media platforms, and local community centers to invite others. A simple post or flyer with details of the walk schedule, meeting points, and your contact information should suffice. Keep your initial group manageable; a cozy number ensures everyone can get to know each other, paving the way for deeper connections.

 Now, onto the fun part: organizing your first meet-up. Choose a safe, accessible location that matches the physical abilities of your group members. Parks, riverwalks, or scenic routes around town are perfect. Plan a short route for your first few walks to accommodate all fitness levels. These initial outings are as much about socializing and setting the club's tone as about exercise. You can vary the routes as your club grows to keep things interesting. Perhaps plan a monthly challenge or a themed walk—like a historical tour of your town—to spice things up.

Walking together isn't just a way to stay fit; it's a step toward building a supportive community. The benefits of joining a walking club stretch beyond the physical. Sure, you're burning calories and strengthening your muscles, but you're also forging friendships. These social interactions can be a significant mood booster, reducing feelings of loneliness and depression. Plus, the rhythmic nature of walking encourages conversation, leading to deeper discussions and a sense of connection that can be hard to find elsewhere.

Safety is paramount, especially when you're responsible for a group. Always check the weather before heading out, and adjust your plans accordingly. Equip yourself with a basic first aid kit for unforeseen scrapes or sprains. Encourage members to wear appropriate footwear and to bring water, especially on warmer days. If your route includes road crossings, remind everyone of road safety rules. Having a mobile phone with you for emergencies is also wise.

Incorporating walking into daily life doesn't require monumental changes. It starts with small steps. Instead of driving to the nearby store, why not walk? Or perhaps take a stroll after dinner instead of heading straight for the couch. These simple choices gradually instill a habit that enhances your lifestyle. For something more structured, how about themed walks? A "Photography Walk" could have members capturing seasonal changes, while a "Nature Walk" focuses on local flora and fauna. These themes make the walks more engaging and encourage participants to see their surroundings through new eyes.

Walking clubs are more than just an excuse to get moving; they are a gateway to enriching your life through shared experiences and connections. Each step strengthens your muscles and communal bonds, enhancing your physical health and social well-being. As you continue to step forward, remember that every walk is a chance to discover, connect, and enjoy the journey at a pace that suits you.

The next chapter will delve into the mental and emotional benefits of engaging in hobbies and activities that stimulate the mind. From puzzles and games to art and music, we'll explore how keeping your brain active is just as crucial as exercising your body, ensuring a well-rounded approach to a joyful and fulfilling retirement.

MENTAL AND EMOTIONAL WELL-BEING

Welcome to the cerebral gymnasium of your retirement! Here, we're not just flexing our muscles but giving our brains a thorough workout. After all, a sharp mind is your best ally in navigating the golden years with wit, wisdom, and perhaps a little humor. Think of this chapter as your personal trainer for mental agility, dishing out fun, games, and a brainy challenge to keep those neurons firing like a well-oiled machine. So, buckle up —or should we say, "think" up—as we dive into the world of brain-boosting hobbies that are more exhilarating than a double espresso on a Monday morning!

BRAIN-BOOSTING HOBBIES: PUZZLES, GAMES, AND MORE

Who said playing games is just child's play? In retirement, puzzles and board games are the secret sauce to keeping your mind as sharp as a tack—or a ninja's sword—if you're into that sort of thing. Engaging regularly in puzzles like Sudoku, crosswords, or even complex jigsaw puzzles can significantly enhance your cognitive functions. It's like taking your brain to the gym, but instead of lifting weights, you're maneuvering through word challenges or strategizing over chess pieces. These activities stimulate neuro-plasticity, which is a fancy way of saying they help your brain adapt and grow, even as you age. They enhance memory, improve problem-solving skills, and can even speed up your cognitive processing. It's like turning your brain into a supercomputer, but thankfully, one that doesn't require software updates or tech support.

Now, let's stock up your mental gym with the best equipment—games known to boost brain health. First on the list is the classic game of chess, which is like the bench press for your brain, enhancing strategic thinking and foresight. Then there's Scrabble, which bolsters your vocabulary and gives your gray matter a fantastic workout as you juggle letters and words in your head, trying to outdo your opponent. For those who prefer going digital, brain-training apps like Lumosity or CogniFit offer a variety of games designed to improve various cognitive skills, from attention to flexibility of thinking. These games are not just entertaining; they're a robust workout schedule for your neurons, ensuring your mental faculties remain in tip-top shape.

But why play alone when you can make it a party? Social gaming opportunities abound, both in person and online, turning what could be a solitary activity into a fun social event. Joining a local bridge or chess club can be a great way to meet new people while keeping your mind engaged. For those who prefer the digital route, online platforms like Tabletopia or Roll20 allow you to play board games virtually with others, offering the double benefit of cognitive stimulation and social interaction. These platforms host an immense variety of games, from the classics to new indie hits, ensuring you always have something exciting to explore with friends, new and old.

Let's discuss hosting the ultimate game night because nothing says "party" like a gathering of friends over strategic conquests and cooperative quests. First, choose games that cater to various skill levels to ensure everyone can participate and enjoy them. Mix it up with cooperative games like Pandemic, where players work together to save the world, and competitive games like Ticket to Ride, which can gently pit friends against one another in a battle of wits and strategy. Make sure your space is comfortable and welcoming, with plenty of seating and good lighting. Provide simple snacks and beverages to keep the gamers happy and hydrated. Lastly, keep the atmosphere light and fun—remember, it's all about enjoyment. A well-planned game night can become a regular event, giving you and your friends something exciting to look forward to and a way to stay connected and mentally active.

In the spirit of combining social interaction with brain-boosting activities, consider forming a club focused on games like Mexican Train Dominoes or Euchre. This engaging endeavor involves gath-  ering friends to rotate hosting duties, where each host's home becomes a vibrant venue for the evening. Participants each contribute an appetizer, creating a potluck atmosphere that is as delightful for the taste buds as the game is for the mind. The setup includes three tables, each accommodating four players, and a set of dominoes (or cards for Euchre), ensuring a dynamic game environment. As the night progresses, players rotate tables after every round. This rotation spices up the competition and maximizes social interaction, allowing each participant to engage with every attendee. This blend of strategy, camaraderie, and culinary sharing creates an ideal scenario for those looking to enrich their social life and cognitive health.

During this vibrant chapter of your retirement life, engaging in brain-boosting activities is about maintaining cognitive functions and enriching your daily life with fun, laughter, and connection. Integrating puzzles, games, and social interactions into your routine means preserving and enhancing your mental health, ensuring that every day is as fulfilling and joyful as possible. So, dust off that chess set, crack open a new jigsaw puzzle, or call up friends for a game night—your brain will thank you, and your retirement will be all the richer for it.

ART AND MUSIC AS THERAPY

Have you ever considered a paintbrush to be a magic wand? Well, in the world of art therapy, it is. Diving into art isn't just about creating something pleasing to the eye; it's a profound journey into self-expression that can sweep away stress like a broom clears cobwebs. When you engage in artistic activities—painting, sculpting, or doodling—you're not just filling a canvas; you're exploring the contours of your inner world. Focusing on colors, shapes, and textures can help quiet the mind, offering a much-needed break from the hustle and bustle of everyday life. It's like giving your brain a "do not disturb" sign, allowing you to disconnect from external pressures and reconnect with yourself.

Think of art as your therapist who doesn't charge by the hour. Creating art can be incredibly cathartic, especially when dealing with emotional baggage. It provides a safe space to express feelings that might be hard to articulate with words. Have you ever felt a sense of relief after scribbling furiously on a piece of paper? That's art therapy's simplest form, helping you release emotions physically and creatively. This expression can lead to significant stress relief and improve overall emotional health. The beauty of art therapy lies in its accessibility; you don't need to be Picasso or

Frida Kahlo to benefit from it. It's about the process, not the product.

Are you interested in exploring your inner Picasso or Georgia O'Keeffe? Getting started with art therapy is easier than you might think. First, gather your essential tools—brushes, paints, paper, or a clay kit if you feel sculptural. The medium isn't as important as the act of creation, so feel free to choose materials you are drawn to. Next, consider joining an art therapy class or workshop. Many community centers, senior centers, and even galleries offer sessions guided by professional art therapists. These classes can provide structured guidance that might be helpful if you're new to the craft. Plus, they offer a chance to meet fellow budding artists, adding a social flavor to your artistic endeavors.

If you aren't into classes, many books and online resources, such as ArtTherapy.org, can help you start your art therapy journey from home. These resources often include prompts and exercises to kickstart your creativity and guide you through the therapeutic process. The key is approaching art therapy with an open mind and heart. It's not about skill; it's about expression and finding peace within the strokes of your creations.

Now, let's tune into another therapy that hits all the right notes— music therapy. If art therapy is a paintbrush, music therapy is a melody that can soothe the soul.

Listening to music or engaging in musical activities has been scientifically proven to elevate mood, reduce anxiety, and even strengthen cognitive functions. Music has a unique way of tapping into our emotions, making it an excellent tool for managing stress and fostering emotional well-being. Whether it's the calming strains of classical music or the upbeat rhythms of rock and roll, each note can resonate with different parts of our psyche, providing comfort and joy.

The therapeutic benefits of music are like a multivitamin for your mental health. It can stimulate brain areas involved in attention, prediction, and memory while reducing those pesky stress hormones. Furthermore, music can elevate your mood by triggering the release of dopamine, that lovely "feel-good" neurotransmitter. So, whether you're belting out tunes in a community choir, strumming a guitar in your living room, or simply tapping your feet to a jazz beat, you're not just enjoying a tune; you're conducting a whole orchestra of neurochemical reactions that boost your mental health.

To weave the therapeutic power of music into your daily life, start by creating playlists that resonate with your various moods and activities—a playlist for relaxing, another for energizing, and maybe one for those moments of nostalgia. Platforms like Spotify and Apple Music make exploring and organizing your favorite tunes easy. Consider starting your day with an uplifting melody or winding down in the evening with smooth jazz or classical music to soothe your soul.

Another delightful way to integrate music into your life is by attending live performances. Whether it's a grand concert hall showcasing a symphony orchestra or a cozy café with a live band, these experiences can be incredibly enriching. The energy of live music isn't just heard; it's felt, reverberating through every cell of your body, energizing your spirit, and soothing your mind. If mobility or availability is a concern, many organizations now offer virtual concerts and performances you can enjoy from your living room. This accessibility ensures that the joy of music remains just a click away, bringing harmony and rhythm into your everyday existence without you having to step outside.

By incorporating art and music into your life, you're not just filling idle time; you're enriching your soul and enhancing your emotional resilience. Each stroke of the brush and each note played adds a layer of joy and peace to your life, proving that therapy doesn't always have to come in a bottle or from a professional's office. It can come from the tip of a brush and the strings of a guitar, weaving beauty and tranquility into the tapestry of your everyday life.

THE POWER OF MEDITATION AND MINDFULNESS

Let's quiet down the chatter in our heads, shall we? Imagine turning down the volume knob on life's stressors just enough so you can hear yourself think or, better yet, enjoy a moment of sweet silence. That's what meditation offers—a mental breather, a retreat from the hustle and bustle of everyday life, right in your living room or wherever you choose to pause and breathe. If you're picturing a monk floating on a cloud of serenity, let's bring it back down to earth. Meditation doesn't require levitation skills or supernatural calm. It's well-grounded in reality, and guess what? It's accessible to everyone, including you.

Meditation is like giving your mind a spa day. It's all about relaxation and rejuvenation, minus the fancy bathrobes and cucumber water. Meditation is simple; it primarily involves focusing your attention and eliminating the stream of jumbled thoughts crowding your mind. Picture it as tuning your radio to a station with tranquil silence instead of the Top 40 chaos. Basic techniques include focusing on your breath, repeating a soothing word or "mantra," or visualizing a serene image. Just as you might start your day with stretching or a cup of coffee, incorporating meditation can awaken your mind, preparing it for the day with clarity and calmness. The perks? Reduced stress, enhanced concentration, better emotional health, and, not to brag, a boost in happiness. It's like discovering the secret to feeling light and breezy, even when your old pal Arthritis comes knocking.

Now, let's sprinkle a little mindfulness into your day. Mindfulness is meditation's outgoing cousin; it's all about being aware and present in the moment. It's noticing the aroma of your morning coffee or the feel of the sun warming your face. Simple exercises can weave mindfulness into your daily routine, transforming mundane activities into moments of Zen. For instance, try the "Five Senses Exercise." Here's how it works: Wherever you are, pause for a moment and notice five things you can see, four things you can touch, three things you can hear, two things you can smell, and one thing you can taste. It's a quick and easy way to center yourself and connect with your environment. Or, when eating, focus on each bite, savoring the flavors and textures. It's a boon for your digestive system and turns a simple meal into a mindful feast.

Feeling intrigued but need help figuring out where to start? The digital world is teeming with resources that can guide you through the valleys and peaks of meditation. Apps like Headspace or Calm offer guided meditations, sleep stories, and mindfulness exercises that cater to beginners and seasoned meditators alike. Would you prefer a more tangible approach? Books such as *Wherever You Go, There You Are* by Jon Kabat-Zinn and *The Miracle of Mindfulness* by Thich Nhat Hanh provide insightful reads on embracing mindfulness in everyday life. Websites like Mindful.org are fantastic resources, offering tips, courses, and articles that make meditation feel as approachable as your morning crossword.

To weave this practice into your life, why not create a special nook in your home dedicated to meditation? It doesn't require renovating your living room; a small, quiet corner will do. Add a comfortable chair or a cushion, perhaps a small table for a candle or incense, and voilà, you have a personal sanctuary. This space should feel tranquil and inviting, a visual reminder to pause and engage in your practice.

As we wrap up this chapter, remember that meditation and mindfulness aren't just about sitting silently or emptying your thoughts; they're vibrant tools for enhancing mental clarity, emotional balance, and well-being. They invite you to experience life more fully, to engage with the present, and to find peace amid the chaos. Whether meditating to find calm, practicing mindfulness to enhance presence, or setting up your little Zen zone, you're taking decisive steps toward a more serene and joyful life.

Next, let's shift gears from the tranquility of mindfulness to the dynamic world of culinary arts. The upcoming chapter will explore how cooking can become a necessity and a delightful hobby that spices up your retirement years with flavors, friendships, and fun. So, grab your apron—we're about to turn up the heat and add some zest to your days!

FOOD FOR THE SOUL—COOKING AND NUTRITION

W elcome to your new favorite room in the house—the kitchen! Gone are the days when cooking felt like a chore, a mere necessity to fuel a body too busy to pause. Retirement gives you the luxury of time, transforming your relationship with the pots and pans into a delightful dance of flavors. Imagine yourself as the maestro of your kitchen, orchestrating ingredients into harmonious symphonies that tantalize the taste buds and nourish the soul. Let's embark on a culinary adventure where every meal is a brushstroke on the canvas of your golden years!

COOKING CLASSES FOR HEALTH AND HAPPINESS

Ditch the microwave meals and fast food—cooking at home is your new best friend. It's healthier, it's cheaper, and, let's be honest, it's way more satisfying. When you cook your meals, you control the ingredients, opting for natural, wholesome options that keep those pesky preservatives at bay. This control is good for your body and a feast for your soul, allowing you to connect with every chop, stir, and sizzle. The act can be meditative and calm in a world that often spins too fast. Plus, let's talk about the wallet—eating out frequently can drain your funds faster than a leaky faucet. Home-cooked meals are kinder to your budget, freeing up more cash for those dream culinary classes or exotic spices to jazz up your dishes.

Now, where to harness this newfound passion? Local cooking classes are a treasure trove of culinary secrets waiting to be unlocked. These classes offer more than just recipes; they're a gateway to new techniques, flavors, and the world's best-kept secret—plating tips that will have your dinner guests wondering if you moonlight as a gourmet chef. Community centers, culinary schools, and even some high-end grocery stores often offer classes tailored for retirees. These classes are designed to be enjoyable and informative, focusing on nutrition that supports a healthy lifestyle as you age. Imagine learning to roll sushi or craft the perfect Italian gnocchi while making friends who share your enthusiasm for good food. It's about feeding your body and social life in one fell swoop.

Only interested in cooking inside your own home? No problem! The digital world is brimming with cooking tutorials, online courses, and forums that bring the culinary school to your living room. YouTube videos are an excellent source of cooking tutorials. Websites like MasterClass or America's Test Kitchen offer video tutorials by celebrity chefs and seasoned cooks who can teach you everything from knife skills to advanced baking techniques. Platforms like these often include community features, allowing you to ask questions and share experiences with fellow home chefs around the globe. It's like having a culinary mentor at the click of a button, ready to guide you through the intricacies of Indian spices or the delicate art of French pastry. Plus, the ability to pause, rewind, and rewatch means you can learn at your own pace without the pressure of keeping up in a live class.

Why keep the joy of cooking to yourself? Turn it into a social event by starting a cooking club or hosting potluck dinners. Imagine a monthly gathering where each friend brings a dish, and together, you share recipes, tips, and a few laughs. Or consider a cooking challenge night, where you pick a theme or ingredient, and everyone cooks their version of a dish featuring that theme. These gatherings are not just about eating; they're about connecting, sharing, and creating memories over shared meals. It's communal dining at its best, turning each meal into an event that nourishes the stomach and the heart.

Cooking is more than just a means to feed the body; it's a way to enrich your life with flavors, friendships, and fulfillment. Each ingredient, each recipe, and each meal is a chapter in the delightful story of your culinary adventures. So, tie on that apron, fire up the stove, and let the magic begin. Your kitchen awaits, ready to be the stage for your next delicious creation.

STARTING A RETIREMENT COOKBOOK CLUB

Imagine turning your love for cooking into a shared adventure with friends by starting a cookbook club. This club is a unique blend of a book club and a dinner party, where cookbooks are the stars and delicious dishes spark engaging conversations. It's not just about eating together; it's an intimate sharing of stories, techniques, and, sometimes, secret ingredients. Creating a cookbook club is more straightforward than it sounds and full of joy. Begin by gathering friends who enjoy cooking and trying new recipes, embracing the fun of kitchen mishaps as stories to share. Set a monthly meeting schedule to give everyone enough time to explore recipes. Choose a diverse cookbook as your first focus, ensuring something for every taste and skill level.

Organizing a meeting is like planning a small event. Use a rotating host system to keep the atmosphere fresh, with the host selecting the cookbook that aligns with the group's tastes. Each member then picks a recipe to prepare for the next gathering, coordinating to ensure a varied menu. During your meetings, discuss the cooking experiences, share personal touches added to the recipes, and celebrate successes and challenges.

Introduce themed gatherings to add creativity, from focusing on specific cuisines to celebrating seasons or holidays. To keep the community spirit alive between meetings, set up a digital platform for members to share photos, tips, and updates to foster a culture of sharing and anticipation for future gatherings. At its core, a cookbook club is about more than just cooking. It's a celebration of friendship, culinary exploration, and the rich tapestry of flavors that make our lives more vibrant. You'll create meaningful connections by sharing recipes, stories, and laughter. So, put on your apron, prepare your palate, and embark on this delightful communal cooking journey.

GARDENING FOR FRESH PRODUCE AND FULFILLMENT

Imagine stepping into your backyard or onto your balcony and plucking a ripe, sun-warmed tomato straight from the vine. Gardening, my friend, is not just about growing plants; it's about cultivating a deeper connection with the cycle of life and, of course, enjoying the literal fruits (and vegetables) of your labor.

Whether you have rolling acres, a modest backyard, or just a few pots on a balcony, starting your garden is a journey back to the basics of nature, and it's easier than you might think.

First things first: Let's talk about setting up your garden. If you're working with limited space or need to keep bending and stretching to a minimum, consider raised beds or container gardening. These options keep everything within arm's reach and can be customized to fit even the smallest spaces. Select the right spot—most vegetables and herbs crave sunlight, so find a place that catches several hours of direct sun daily.

Next, pick your plants. For beginners, it's wise to start with something hearty and forgiving, like herbs, lettuce, or radishes. They're almost like the pet rocks of the gardening world—hard to mess up and sure to give back some love. Once you've chosen your plants, it's all about the soil. A rich, organic potting mix will nourish your plants from the get-go. With these elements in place, you're well on your way to harvesting a bumper crop right from your little patch of green.

Now, while your green babies are growing, let's chew over the health benefits of gardening. It's a fantastic physical activity for maintaining flexibility, strength, and stamina. But its benefits spill over into mental health territory, too. Gardening is a stress reliever; it's meditative and mindful, connecting you to the rhythms of nature, which, in turn, can help soothe frazzled nerves. Plus, there's nothing quite like the satisfaction of seeing your plants thrive—a boost to self-esteem and a balm for the soul. And let's not overlook the nutritional aspect. Fresh produce from your garden is not just tastier; it's packed with nutrients and free from the dubious charms of pesticides and long-haul transportation.

Community gardens are a fantastic option for those who crave more social interaction or want to scale up their gardening ambitions. These communal spaces offer a chance to cultivate plants and friendships alike. Many community gardens provide plots you can rent and manage, along with shared tools and resources. It's a great way to connect with neighbors and fellow gardening enthusiasts, share tips and tricks, and, sometimes, swap produce. Plus, community gardens often engage in food donation programs, allowing you to help provide fresh produce to those in need.

Let's not forget the culinary delights that come with a garden. Cooking with home-grown ingredients isn't just a gourmet flex; it's a full-circle moment in your food journey. Imagine whipping up a salad with greens you grew yourself or garnishing a dish with fresh herbs plucked right before dinner. And if you find yourself with a surplus, why not try preserving it? Canning, freezing, and drying extend your garden's bounty throughout the year. Opening a jar of homemade tomato sauce in the middle of winter is profoundly satisfying, a vibrant reminder of summer's warmth.

Gardening, in all its forms, invites you to slow down and reconnect with the nurturing side of nature. It's about growing food, beautifying spaces, sharing with neighbors, and enriching your physical and mental well-being. Whether you're a seasoned green thumb or a budding novice, each seed you plant is a step toward a healthier, more connected life. So, grab those gardening gloves and get ready to dig deep, not just into the soil but also into a fulfilling new chapter that brings growth in more ways than one.

As we wrap up this exploration into the verdant world of gardening, remember that each plant nurtured is not just a step toward self-sufficiency but a leap toward living sustainably. The simple acts of planting, tending, and harvesting connect us to the rhythms of nature and remind us of our role within these cycles. From the quiet solitude of early morning watering to the joyous community harvests, gardening enriches our lives, providing food for the body and solace for the soul.

Looking ahead, we'll turn from the earthy gardening pursuits to the digital domains of modern technology. In the next chapter, we'll explore how embracing technology can enhance your retirement, offering new avenues for connection, learning, and entertainment. Ready to swap your spade for a smartphone? Let's see what tech-savvy treasures await!

EMBRACING TECHNOLOGY

T he wonderful world of technology! We touched on it earlier
in the book but need to dive deeper. Once the realm of whiz
kids and Silicon Valley types, technology is now a playground for
savvy retirees like yourself, eager to tweet, swipe, and scroll with
the best of them. Gone are the days when a phone was just a
phone. Today, it's your camera, library, navigator, and—let's be
honest—sometimes your best friend. Stepping into the digital age
is like dancing the tango: it's all about learning the steps, but once
you get the hang of it, it's an exhilarating whirl that keeps you
connected and engaged. So, let's power up and dive into the
sparkling digital waters where smartphones and tablets await to
guide you in this thrilling chapter of your life.

MASTERING SMARTPHONES AND TABLETS

Remember when staying in touch meant rotary phones and snail
mail? Fasten your seatbelt because smartphones and tablets have
turbocharged how we connect. These devices are not just phones
and notepads; they're your gateway to the world. With a few taps,

you can video call your grandkids, text your golf buddy about the next game, or send a photo of your latest adventure straight to family and friends. Apps like WhatsApp, FaceTime, Zoom, and Skype have revolutionized communication, making it easier than ever to stay in the loop. Whether you're scheduling a family reunion or just saying a quick hello, these tools ensure that distance no longer dictates the dynamics of your relationships. Imagine watching your grandson's first steps live through your screen or celebrating your sister's birthday via a video call. No matter how small, each connection helps weave a tighter web of family and friendship, keeping you close to the hearts of those you love, no matter where they roam.

Now, let's talk apps because your smartphone is only as good as the apps it holds. Think of apps as tools in a Swiss Army knife, each serving a specific purpose to make your life easier, healthier, or more fun. For health, apps like MyFitnessPal can help track your nutrition, while Headspace offers guided meditations to calm your mind. For daily activities, consider Evernote for notetaking or Wunderlist for managing your to-do lists. And let's not forget entertainment; apps like Audible for audiobooks or Spotify for music can fill your days with culture and tunes with just a tap. The appropriate set of apps can turn your device into a personal assistant, entertainment center, and health coach all rolled into one. It's about customizing your digital experience to fit your life-style, so explore the App Store or Google Play and start tailoring your tech to meet your needs.

But what good are all these apps if you can't find them? Customizing your device for ease of use is like setting up your living room so everything you need is within easy reach. Most smartphones and tablets allow you to adjust settings to suit your preferences. Increase the font size so you're not squinting, orga-nize your apps so your favorites are on the home screen, and adjust the brightness to a comfortable level. If you fumble over touch screens, explore settings that enhance touch sensitivity or use voice commands to control your device. Remember, your device is there to serve you, not to challenge your patience. Spend some time tweaking these settings, and transform your smartphone or tablet into a friend, not a foe.

Updating your device is like giving it a regular health check— ensuring everything runs smoothly and securely. Software updates often include security enhancements that protect your data from new threats, along with improvements that make your device faster or more efficient. They can also introduce new features that enhance your experience, ensuring you get the most out of your technology. Think of it as a tune-up for your car; it might be a bit of a hassle, but it keeps everything running smoothly in the long run. So, when that little update notification pops up, don't procrastinate. Please take a few minutes to install the update; your digital life will thank you.

Navigating the world of smartphones and tablets might seem daunting at first. Still, with the proper setup, curiosity, and a willingness to experiment, you'll find they open a world of possibilities. From staying connected with loved ones to managing your daily tasks, these devices offer countless tools to enhance your life. So, embrace the tech, explore its potential, and remember, there's no age limit on digital savvy—it's just another part of your journey, ready to be mastered with a touch, a swipe, and maybe just a little bit of patience.

NAVIGATING SOCIAL MEDIA SAFELY

Diving into the digital world of social media can feel like stepping into a bustling city; it's vibrant and exciting but also requires a bit of street-smart savvy to navigate safely. Think of each social media platform as a different neighborhood. With its community groups and event pages, Facebook is like the town square where everyone meets to catch up, share news, and join clubs. Here, you can reconnect with old friends, join groups based on your interests, or even follow pages that offer daily inspiration, whether gardening, cooking, or DIY crafts. On the other hand, Instagram is the trendy art district—the place to share your latest photos, whether they're snapshots of your garden blooms or culinary triumphs. It's visual storytelling at its best—a way to communicate your adventures and creations, capturing moments in time with a single click.

While these platforms offer excellent avenues for connection and expression, they also require cautious navigation. Let's start with privacy settings—a crucial step to ensuring your online experience is fun and safe. Consider privacy settings as your personal security system, keeping your digital house  safe. Each platform has its own settings, and taking the time to understand and adjust them is critical. You can decide who sees your posts, who can contact you, and even manage which ads you see. On Facebook, for instance, you can customize your post visibility to be public, friends-only, or even visible to only specific people. Similarly, Instagram lets you make your account private, meaning only approved followers can see your posts. Adjusting these settings isn't just about safeguarding your privacy; it's about creating a space where you feel comfortable to share and engage without worries.

Engaging with online communities is another vibrant aspect of social media that can enrich your digital experience. Whether you are a knitting enthusiast or a vintage car aficionado, there's a community for you. These platforms can be excellent resources for connecting with people who share your interests, offering a sense of belonging and an endless exchange of ideas and support. Engaging effectively in these communities means more than just lurking on the sidelines; it's about contributing to conversations, sharing your experiences, and supporting others. Participation is the bridge that turns casual browsing into meaningful interaction. However, it's essential to engage wisely—be respectful, stay positive, and avoid sharing too much personal information. Remember, the goal is to build connections and learn from each other in a safe and supportive environment.

Sharing safely is the golden rule of social media. In the excitement of sharing moments, thinking twice before posting is crucial. Avoid sharing personal information like your home address, financial details, or anything else that could compromise your safety. Be cautious about posting photos that might reveal more than intended, especially when it involves grandchildren or family events. A good rule of thumb is to ask yourself, "Would I share this information on a billboard?" If the answer is no, it's probably not wise to share it online. Additionally, be mindful of the information you share about others. Always seek permission before posting pictures of friends or family, ensuring you respect their privacy.

Navigating social media safely is about embracing the benefits while understanding the risks. By choosing the right platforms, setting your privacy controls, engaging thoughtfully with communities, and sharing wisely, you can enjoy a rich and rewarding online experience. Social media opens a world of connection and discovery, and with the proper precautions, you can easily explore this digital landscape with confidence and ease.

ONLINE LEARNING: FROM LANGUAGES TO PHOTOGRAPHY

The digital era has flung open the doors to learning opportunities that once required hefty textbooks and stern-faced professors. Now, the world of knowledge is just a click away, allowing you to dive deep into subjects that tickle your fancy from the comfort of your favorite armchair. Whether you dream of conversing fluently in Italian or capturing breathtaking photographs, online learning platforms are treasure chests full of the jewels of knowledge just waiting to be unearthed by enthusiastic minds like yours.

Let's paint a picture of the vast landscape of online education. Platforms such as Udemy, Coursera, and Khan Academy are like bustling marketplaces of old, where scholars and apprentices gathered to exchange wisdom. Udemy offers a kaleidoscope of courses, ranging from web development to personal development and everything in between. It's your go-to if you want to pick up practical skills, perhaps to finally start that blog or master the art of watercolor painting. The Coursera platform partners with leading universities and companies worldwide to bring you courses that are a tad more academic, often complete with certificates that sparkle nicely on your virtual mantelpiece. Khan Academy, on the other hand, is the place to brush up on those rusty school subjects like math, science, or economics, all for free. Each platform has its own unique flavor, so taste-testing a few can help you decide which suits your learning palate the best.

Now, embarking on an educational adventure requires preparation. Setting realistic learning goals is like plotting your route on a map before a big trip. Begin by asking yourself what you want to achieve. Is your goal to learn Spanish well enough to chat with locals on your next trip to Spain? Or perhaps you want to understand the basics of digital photography before your grandchild's wedding? Once you've pinpointed your objectives, break them down into bite-sized milestones. If Spanish is your goal, start with basic vocabulary and grammar, gradually building up to more complex conversations. For photography, you might begin with understanding your camera settings, then move on to composition, and, finally, advanced lighting techniques.

Creating a study schedule that fits into your retirement life is crucial. Unlike traditional school, there's no bell to signal the start of class, so discipline is critical. Allocate specific times of the day for your studies. Maybe you're a morning person, and absorbing new information is best done with your first cup of coffee. Or perhaps you're a night owl, and evenings are when you feel most inspired. Whichever it is, consistency is your friend. Aim to dedicate at least a few hours each week to your studies. Flexibility is one of the perks of retirement and online learning, so adjusting your schedule is okay if life throws you a curveball. The goal is to keep learning enjoyable, not overwhelming.

The benefits of diving into lifelong learning are vast. Beyond the gain of acquiring new knowledge and skills, engaging your brain in learning can significantly enhance cognitive function. It keeps the gears in your mind well-oiled and running smoothly, much like regular exercise does for your body. But even more beautifully, learning new skills can open doors to new social connections. Imagine joining a photography club or a language exchange group. These new ventures allow you to share your passions and discoveries with others, creating meaningful interactions and friendships. Every new skill you acquire is a key to a new community, conversation, and way of seeing the world.

As you continue to explore the rich and varied offerings of online learning, remember that each lesson learned, each skill mastered, is a step toward a more fulfilled and vibrant life. The opportunities are limitless, and the benefits are boundless. So why not seize them with both hands and a curious mind, transforming these golden years into a time of growth, connection, and discovery?

VIRTUAL REALITY FOR THE MORE TECHNOLOGICALLY ADVENTUROUS

Picture this: One moment, you're in your living room, and the next, you're walking the streets of Paris or diving into the Great Barrier Reef—all from the comfort of your favorite armchair. Welcome to the virtual reality (VR) world, a technology not just for the young or gamers but for anyone with a zest for life and an appetite for adventure. VR offers a doorway to worlds both real and imagined. For retirees, it presents a unique opportunity to break the boundaries of everyday experience and rediscover the thrill of exploration and learning.

Virtual reality operates through devices like headsets and controllers that immerse you in an astonishingly realistic digital environment. Imagine donning a headset, and suddenly, you're not just looking at a screen but part of the scene. This immersion sets VR apart from traditional computing or television viewing—it's an interactive experience that engages your senses to a degree that's often startling in its intensity. For retirees, the benefits go beyond just the wow factor. VR can be a tool for enhanced physical activity, social interaction, and cognitive engagement. It can transport you to new places, offering travel and exploration without needing luggage or tickets. It can also provide mental challenges that keep your mind sharp, like navigating new environments or solving puzzles in a three-dimensional space. Moreover, VR experiences can be shared; you could explore ancient Greece's ruins while your friend, miles away, joins you on the same adventure, providing fun and a new way to spend quality time with loved ones.

Navigating the market for VR devices might seem daunting at first, but it all boils down to finding what works best for your lifestyle and interests. The Oculus Quest 2, for example, is a user-friendly standalone headset known for its high-quality graphics and ease of use. It doesn't require a connection to a computer or a complicated setup, only access to Wi-Fi, making it a good choice for those who prefer straightforward technology. Another excellent option is the HTC Vive, which offers precise tracking and high-resolution displays for a deeply immersive experience. For those who own a PlayStation 4, the PlayStation VR is a cost-effective way to step into virtual reality without additional heavy investments.

Purchasing a VR device is just the beginning. Setting it up correctly is crucial to ensuring the best experience. Most VR headsets come with a setup guide that walks you through the process, which usually involves adjusting the headset for comfort and clarity, setting up sensors and boundaries if needed, and connecting to any apps or platforms that enhance your VR experience. Retailers like Best Buy often offer setup services, or you can ask a tech-savvy friend or family member to help. Online tutorials can also be invaluable, offering step-by-step visual guides to get you started.

Once your device is up and running, the real fun begins. Dive into the world of VR apps and games. Platforms like SteamVR, Oculus Store, and PlayStation Store offer a wide range of VR content, from passive experiences like virtual tours of foreign cities and museums to more active engagements like puzzle games, sports simulations, and interactive stories. Whether exploring the ocean depths, touring a virtual art gallery, or learning a new skill, VR can bring it all to life with stunning realism.

As you embrace this cutting-edge technology, remember that the virtual reality world is vast and varied. Each experience offers fun and entertainment and provides a unique way to engage with content that can stimulate your mind, challenge your body, and enrich your social life. Virtual reality is not just a gateway to new experiences—it's a new way to experience life, offering endless learning, exploring, and connecting possibilities.

As we close this chapter on embracing technology, from mastering smartphones to diving into the virtual worlds of VR, it's clear that technology offers many ways to enhance your life. Each device, each platform, and each app open new avenues for connection, exploration, and entertainment. Technology in retirement is not just about keeping up with the times; it's about enriching your golden years with experiences that keep you engaged, connected, and continuously learning. So, as you move forward, carry with you the curiosity to explore, the openness to learn, and the wisdom to navigate this digital age with confidence and joy. Next, we journey into the world of travel and exploration, where we bring the adventurous spirit into the tangible world, exploring new landscapes, cultures, and experiences that await your next chapter of discovery.

Join Me on My Mission!

"Often when you think you're at the end of something, you're at the beginning of something else."

— FRED ROGERS

When you've spent every day of your adult life governed by a work schedule and all the pressures that come with it, the vast expanse of free time you're suddenly faced with when you enter retirement can be overwhelming. It certainly was for me, and I realized I had to make a conscious effort to fill it with things that would bring me joy to ensure that I continued to live a full life and reap all the rewards my working years had brought me.

I've met plenty of people who found this more difficult than I did —many of them commenting on how some weeks, the days seem to blur and they looked back not really sure what they'd done with their time. To me, this seems like a tragic waste, and for some people, it doesn't get better, and they end up filling their days with crossword puzzles, allowing time to slip away without finding ways to the richness and fulfillment that retirement can offer. I wrote this book in the hope of helping more people make sure this doesn't happen to them. Retirement is a beautiful opportunity to do all the things you've always wanted to do, to discover new interests and passions, and to continue to grow and develop as a person.

I know you see this opportunity—if you didn't, you wouldn't have picked up this book. I hope you're already collecting ideas and thinking about how you can use these years ahead of you to enrich your life, and I'd like to invite you to help me on my mission to make sure that retirement is a fulfilling time for as many people as

I can. It's easier than you might think—all you have to do is leave a short review.

By leaving a review of this book on Amazon, you'll point new readers in the direction of the advice they're looking for when they're searching for help to make sure their retirement years are the best years of their lives.

Much as we all look forward to retirement, it's a daunting prospect, and there are many people actively searching for guidance. Your review will help them find it easily and make their transition into retirement as rich and rewarding as possible.

Thank you so much for your support. You're already using your retirement for good!

Scan the QR code below to leave your review.

TRAVEL AND EXPLORATION

Once the exclusive realm of the jet-setters and the backpack-clad youth, it has now gloriously expanded to include those of us sporting a few more wrinkles and a wealth of stories. Retirement is not the time to plant your feet firmly on the porch but rather the perfect opportunity to dust off the old suitcase and set forth on adventures that would make Marco Polo tip his hat in respect. Forget the mundane routine of daily life; the world is your oyster, and it's high time to savor its pearls, one destination at a time.

EXPLORING THE RV LIFESTYLE

For retirees eager to explore through the windshield of an RV, life on the road can be an excellent way to travel while keeping costs under control. But before you dive headfirst into the RV lifestyle, here are a few pieces of advice to help you enjoy your adventures while staying safe and feeding your wanderlust without breaking the bank.

First, choose the most appropriate recreational vehicle for you. Start by selecting an RV that fits your budget and needs. Consider a used RV to save money, but ensure it has been well-maintained to avoid costly repairs. Look for models with low mileage, and research various manufacturers to under-  stand the options. Class B motorhomes and travel trailers are often more affordable and economical than larger Class A motorhomes.

Plan your route and campground stays before you leave home. Preplanning your travel route can help you find the most afford- able campgrounds and RV parks. Look for free or low-cost camping options like those offered by state parks, national forests, and Bureau of Land Management (BLM) lands. Websites like Campendium and FreeCampsites.net can be valuable resources for finding these spots.

The US National Parks and Federal Recreational Lands Senior Pass is a popular option for U.S. citizens 62 and older who want to enjoy the nation's public lands at a discounted rate. A lifetime Senior Pass, valid for the rest of your life, can be purchased for $80 (at the time of this writing) or $20 for an annual pass. This pass provides free access to more than 2,000 federal recreation sites.

Army Corps of Engineers (USACE) parks are public recreational areas managed by the U.S. Army Corps of Engineers, a federal agency under the Department of Defense. These parks are typi- cally located near water bodies such as lakes, rivers, and reser- voirs that the Corps has built or manages. USACE offers passes like the America the Beautiful Pass, an interagency pass that provides access to more than 2,000 federal recreation sites, including USACE parks. Holders of this pass may receive discounts on fees. USACE also offers Senior and Access Passes that offer significant discounts on fees for U.S. citizens or permanent residents who are 62 years of age or older or for those with permanent disabilities.

You can also save significantly by joining RV Clubs and other memberships. Investing in an RV club membership can yield significant savings on campground fees, fuel, and other travel-related expenses. Clubs like Good Sam, Passport America, and Escapees offer discounts nationwide at numerous RV parks and campgrounds. The Family Motor Coach Association (FMCA) offers memberships of varying levels, which provide discounts, many benefits, and online RV education.

Regular maintenance of your RV is crucial for avoiding unexpected repair costs. Stick to a maintenance schedule for essential systems like the engine, brakes, and tires. Learning to perform basic maintenance tasks can save money and ensure your RV stays in good shape.

Establishing a budget for your RV travels can help you manage your finances effectively. Track all expenses, including fuel, food, campground fees, and entertainment. Use budgeting apps like RV Life Pro, Roadtrippers, or simple spreadsheets to monitor your spending and adjust as needed to stay within your limits.

While on the road, adopt a frugal lifestyle to stretch your budget further. Cook meals in your RV instead of dining out, take advantage of senior discounts, and seek out free or low-cost attractions and activities. Many communities offer free events, and nature provides endless opportunities for inexpensive recreation like hiking, fishing, and birdwatching. By carefully planning your travels, choosing the right RV, and adopting a thrifty mindset, you can enjoy the freedom and adventure of the RV lifestyle without breaking the bank.

PLANNING YOUR SOLO ADVENTURE

Imagine this: You, alone with your thoughts, meandering through the cobblestone streets of a sleepy Italian village or sipping coffee at a quaint Parisian café, watching the world whirl by. Solo travel is not just about changing your location; it's about changing your perspective. It's a splendid way to meet yourself again, away from the roles you've played—parent, spouse, employee. Here, you are just you, unadorned and free to explore the world and your place within it—solo travel strips away the familiar, presenting challenges that foster growth and resilience. You'll learn to navigate foreign cities, communicate despite language barriers, and make decisions independently. Each day is a fresh page in your personal story, written by you and starring you.

However, traveling solo requires a dollop of caution with your daring. Safety is paramount, particularly in unfamiliar lands. Always ensure someone back home knows your itinerary and checks in regularly. Embrace technology for safety; apps like TripWhistle Global SOS provide emergency phone numbers for police, fire, and medical services worldwide. Be mindful of your surroundings, especially at night, and trust your instincts—if something feels off, it probably is. Keep copies of essential documents like your passport and insurance in separate locations, and make digital copies accessible online. Remember, a safe traveler is a happy traveler!

Packing for solo travel is an art form where less is more. The last thing you want is to wrestle with oversized luggage on a crowded train or navigate narrow streets with a suitcase that's half your size. Opt for versatility and mobility; a durable, well-sized backpack might just become your best travel companion. Pack clothes that can be layered and mixed to fit various climates and cultural norms. Essentials include a good pair of walking shoes, a versatile jacket, and quick-dry items. Don't forget a small medical kit, chargers, and universal adapters. A handy tip: roll your clothes to save space and avoid wrinkles. Every inch of your suitcase is prime real estate, so choose wisely! Plus, although most carriers will allow two free suitcases when flying from the United States, this is not the case when traveling back to the States. You don't want to be surprised when that extra suitcase costs 100 euros as you check your luggage to return home.

Selecting the right destination is crucial, especially when you're flying solo. Look for places known for their safety, accessibility, and friendly locals. Countries like New Zealand, Portugal, and Japan score highly. Consider your interests—history buffs might gravitate toward Rome or Athens, while nature lovers could explore the national parks of Canada or the beaches of Costa Rica. Check travel forums, blogs, and senior travel groups for insights and suggestions. They can offer a wealth of information and first-hand experiences that guide you toward beautiful and welcoming destinations for solo travelers. Remember, the best places dazzle your eyes and comfort your soul.

Embarking on a solo adventure is an exhilarating blend of freedom, self-discovery, and unscripted moments. It's about embracing independence, cherishing the solitude that comes with it, and returning home with a trove of memories and a deeper understanding of the world and yourself. So, take that leap—plan, pack, and set forth into the great wide somewhere. After all, the stories you'll tell and the experiences you'll cherish are waiting on the other side of your front door, ready to accompany you on this magnificent solo voyage.

GROUP TRAVEL OPPORTUNITIES FOR RETIREES

Who says adventure is a young person's game? Group travel tours for retirees are like summer camps for grown-ups but with better accommodations and less questionable cafeteria food. It's all about exploring new territories with a band of like-minded explorers who remember the Beatles in their heyday or understand the importance of a good nap. Finding a suitable group travel tour is more than just signing up for the first option on your Google search. It involves some detective work to ensure the trip caters specifically to the senior crowd, focusing on your comfort, interests, and pace. Start by visiting travel agencies that specialize in senior travel. These folks understand that you might want to admire the Sistine Chapel without rushing through it like there's a two-for-one sale at the Vatican. Websites like Road Scholar or ElderTreks design tours with seniors in mind, offering everything from cultural immersion to wildlife adventures, all paced just right for you to savor the experience rather than rush through it.

The benefits of threading through the cobblestones of Europe or the jungles of South America with a group are plentiful. For starters, there's the camaraderie. Traveling with a group means you're never alone, making it easier to enjoy shared experiences that turn into cherished memories. Whether marveling at a sunset over the Sahara or tasting a perfect spaghetti carbonara in Rome, these moments become richer when shared.

Moreover, group tours often come with expert guides who not only know the history of the Colosseum but can also tell you which gelato shop nearby is the best. And let's not forget the convenience factor—group tours handle all the logistics, from airport transfers to hotel bookings, so you can focus on enjoying your trip rather than fretting over the details.

Selecting the appropriate tour is crucial to ensuring your adventure is delightful rather than draining. Look for tours that balance sightseeing with ample downtime. Your vacation shouldn't feel like a race. Check the itinerary for travel times; spending every other day on a bus can be taxing. Make sure there are opportunities for leisurely dining, perhaps a nice afternoon café stop or a leisurely evening stroll in a scenic locale, where the pace is relaxed, and the dining is not just a necessity but a part of the cultural experience. Accommodations are equally important; ensure that hotels are comfortable and conveniently located. Nobody wants to trek across town after an invigorating day of sightseeing. Lastly, consider the size of the group. Smaller groups tend to offer a more personal experience, making it easier to forge friendships and receive individual attention from the tour guide.

Speaking of making connections, group trips are fertile ground for cultivating new friendships, as shared experiences are a fantastic icebreaker. One day, you're strangers; the next, you're swapping stories about your grandchildren or discussing your favorite novels. To foster these connections, engage actively with your fellow travelers. Join in on group activities, share meals, or propose a group photo. These interactions enrich the travel experience, creating bonds forged by shared adventures and mutual discoveries. Who knows? You might find your next travel buddy for future escapades.

In essence, group travel for retirees isn't just about seeing new places; it's about experiencing them in a way that suits your pace, sparks your interest, and satisfies your desire for adventure and comfort. It's about building friendships and memories that enrich your golden years, making every trip not just a departure from the every day but a meaningful journey into the heart of what makes life truly vibrant.

VOLUNTOURISM: COMBINING TRAVEL WITH GIVING BACK

Welcome to the enriching world of voluntourism, where the spirit of adventure meets the heart of service. We have touched on this topic several times throughout the book, but its numerous advantages warrant more discussion. Imagine swapping the typical tourist spots for a hands-on project that immerses you in a local community, where you're not just passing through but making a tangible difference. Voluntourism blends the thrill of travel with the fulfilling experience of helping others, turning a regular holiday into a transformative journey for you and the community you choose to support.

Voluntourism offers a unique opportunity to engage with the world more meaningfully. It's about putting your skills, energy, and compassion to work in environments that may lack resources but abound in gratitude and warmth. Whether it's teaching English in a remote village, helping with wildlife conservation, or building homes in underdeveloped areas, each voluntourism project invites you to step into a local setting that offers a deeper understanding of the people and challenges of that area. This kind of travel allows you to connect with cultures on a level that typical tourism can't match, offering insights and experiences that are both humbling and enriching.

When selecting a voluntourism project, aligning your choice with your values and interests is crucial. Start by assessing what you're passionate about. Are you moved by educational initiatives, environmental conservation, or community development? Your project should resonate with your personal ethos to ensure your efforts feel rewarding and impactful. Research organizations that align with your interests and evaluate their reputation and the support they provide to volunteers. Organizations should be transparent about where contributions go and the direct impact of volunteer efforts.

In early 2024, I embarked on a week-long journey of volunteering at a wildlife conservation center in Zimbabwe named Imire. This opportunity, priced at an all-inclusive rate of USD 950 for seven nights, covered accommodations, all meals, and daily safari game drives in exchange for assistance behind the scenes. This arrangement presented an affordable means to immerse in the African Safari experience. It allowed for close encounters with elephants and rhinos and provided insight into the conservation center's operations. The highlight was participating in an emergency rhino operation, a truly once-in-a-lifetime experience.

The benefits of such engagements extend beyond the tangible contributions to the host communities. For you, the traveler, it's a chance to develop new skills, gain unique insights into global issues, and experience personal growth that only comes from stepping out of your comfort zone. The bonds formed with fellow volunteers and locals can last a lifetime, providing a profound sense of global connectivity.

For those ready to explore voluntourism, several reputable agencies offer structured programs to ensure safety, comfort, and impact. Conservation Travel Africa focuses on wildlife and rural community projects, offering a chance to work closely with Africa's majestic wildlife and support conservation efforts. Global Vision International provides a variety of projects, from teaching to environmental conservation, with comprehensive support tailored to older volunteers. ElderTreks, another excellent agency, offers small group adventures worldwide for people over 50, focusing on cultural immersion and local community impact, perfect for those who want a mix of adventure and altruism.

Preparing for your trip involves practical considerations to ensure a successful experience. Research the health and safety recommendations for your destination—vaccinations, travel insurance, and safety protocols are all must-haves. Pack appropriately for the work and climate—durable clothing and sturdy shoes are essentials. Learn as much as possible about the local culture and customs before you go; showing respect and cultural sensitivity is critical to a positive experience. Lastly, maintain an open mind and a flexible attitude—voluntourism often requires adapting to unforeseen challenges and changes.

As we wrap up this chapter on the transformative power of travel combined with giving back, remember that each destination offers a unique opportunity to see the world and make a meaningful impact. Now, as we turn the page, let's explore the lifelong learning opportunities where education continues to shape our golden years, bringing us joy and new challenges.

LIFELONG LEARNING BEYOND THE CLASSROOM

Retirement is the time when no more alarm clocks blare at the crack of dawn, no more mind-numbing meetings about meetings take place, and, indeed, there is no more racing to beat the 5 p.m. traffic. But wait, before settling into that comfy recliner for a marathon of daytime soaps, consider this: Your brain might be itching for a bit more stimulation than your television can provide. Fear not, because the world of documentaries and podcasts is here to transform your lazy afternoons into a riveting cinema of the mind, packed with all the intrigue, drama, and educational tidbits one could hope for.

DOCUMENTARIES AND PODCASTS FOR THE CURIOUS MIND

Exploring Documentaries

Imagine this: one minute, you're in your living room, and the next, you're traversing the vast savannas of Africa or uncovering the secrets of the ocean's deepest trenches—all from the comfort of your favorite armchair. Welcome to documentaries, where reality is more fascinating than fiction. Documentaries have this magical way of whisking you away to different times and places while keeping your intellect engaged and your curiosity piqued. They are not just films; they are windows to the world, offering insights into topics as diverse as history, science, culture, and technology.

But where do you find these captivating films? Streaming platforms like Netflix and Amazon Prime have become the modern-day treasure chests for documentary enthusiasts. You can access various movies and series covering every imaginable topic with just a few clicks. For the history buffs, *The World at War* offers a thorough and engaging look at World War II. If nature calls to you, *Planet Earth* paints breathtaking portraits of Earth's diverse natural environments. For those intrigued by the complexities of the human mind, *Making a Murderer* provides a gritty exploration of the American legal system. Each documentary entertains and educates, leaving you a little wiser at the credits roll. And don't forget *TED Talks*. Listening to *TED Talks* offers the benefit of gaining insights and inspiration from leading experts across diverse fields, enabling personal growth, and expanding your understanding of various topics.

But let's not forget about the ears—podcasts are here to fill your kitchen or walk in the park with voices that inform, entertain, and sometimes provoke. Think of podcasts as radio shows on demand, discussing everything under the sun, from the intricacies of politics to the light-hearted banter about gardening. But with over two million podcasts floating around the internet, how do you fish out the ones worth your time?

Here's a little tip: Start with your interests. Apps like Spotify, Apple Podcasts, and Google Podcasts are the gateways to finding shows that tickle your fancy. Use the search function to explore topics you're curious about, and don't forget to check the reviews and ratings, as they can guide you to quality content. If technology is your jam, *Reply All* explores modern life and technology in an insightful and often humorous way. Or maybe you're a history lover; *Hardcore History* by Dan Carlin presents historical events in a profoundly engaging and detailed manner. Remember, every podcast episode is an opportunity to learn something new, so plug in those headphones and let the learning begin.

Now, if you're wondering how to access all this content, let's talk about leveraging streaming services like Netflix, YouTube, and Hulu. These platforms are not just for watching sitcom reruns or the latest blockbuster hits. They are rich with educational content disguised as entertainment. Searching for docu-mentaries or educational series on these platforms can be as fruitful as a squirrel's autumn nut-gathering escapade. And the best part? You can learn at your own pace and on your schedule. No need to rush through traffic to make it to a lecture on time!

Lastly, passive-watching or listening is OK, but why not kick it up a notch? Engage with the content you consume. Found a documentary on Roman history fascinating? Pull out a map and trace the borders of the ancient empire. Are you intrigued by a podcast on climate change? Start a journal about making daily changes to help the environment. Discussion forums, online book clubs, and even social media groups can offer platforms to discuss and dissect the topics that pique your interest. Engaging actively with what you learn solidifies your knowledge and makes the process more enjoyable and meaningful.

In the grand theater of your retirement, documentaries and podcasts play leading roles in keeping your mind sharp, curious, and hungry for knowledge. They transform the ordinary into the extraordinary, proving that learning doesn't stop when work does —instead, it blossoms, offering new insights and joys in the autumn of life. So, continue to explore, question, and learn. After all, every day is a new opportunity to add another fascinating fact to your arsenal of dinner party conversation starters.

JOINING A BOOK CLUB OR WRITING WORKSHOP

If you are like me, you long to curl up with a good book—whether it's a thrilling mystery, a swooning romance, or a brain-bending science fiction saga, books can transport us to different worlds. But why journey through these literary landscapes alone when you can share the adventure with a club full of fellow book enthusiasts? Yes, I'm talking about book clubs—those wonderful gatherings where wine often flows as freely as discussions and where the pages of a book open doors to deeper human connections.

The beauty of book clubs lies not just in the shared love of reading but in the vibrant discussions that spring forth from each page. In book clubs, characters and plots are dissected with surgical precision, and personal perceptions are broadened through group insights. Imagine the lively debates over Colleen Hoover's latest psychological thriller or on the opposite end of the spectrum, the collective awe shared while unraveling the fantastical worlds of *The Hobbit*. Each meeting is an opportunity to see the world through a new lens, broadening your understanding and appreciation of literature. At the same time, the sense of community helps build relationships that enrich your social life in meaningful ways.

Starting your book club is like planting a garden of ideas and watching it bloom. Begin by inviting friends, neighbors, or acquaintances who share your passion for books, or put up a notice at your local library or bookstore to attract fellow readers. Choose books that will spark interest and discussion—varying genres and themes—to keep the engagement high. As the host, your role is to facilitate discussions, ensuring everyone gets a chance to voice their thoughts and keeping the conversation flowing and on topic. You might even theme your gatherings around the book's setting—think tea and scones for a British classic or tapas for a Spanish tale—adding layers of fun and authenticity to your meetings.

If you enjoy wielding a pen (or keyboard), writing workshops could be your stage. These workshops are a fantastic way for budding or seasoned writers to hone their craft, receive constructive feedback, and meet fellow wordsmiths. Whether you dream of crafting the next great American novel or want to capture your life's stories for your grandchildren, writing workshops provide the tools and support to help you translate your thoughts into the written word.

Finding a workshop that suits your needs can be as simple as a quick internet search or visiting local community centers and colleges, which often offer writing courses. Many seminars are now available online, offering the flexibility to participate from anywhere at any time. These platforms guide you through the technical aspects of writing—such as structure, style, and pacing—and offer the chance to engage with an online community of writers. Online seminars can be enriching, especially when you are stuck or need encouragement.

Sharing your personal stories through writing serves as a cathartic exercise. It leaves a legacy for future generations—a way for them to connect with you through your words and experiences. Writing about your life isn't just about recording events; it's about reflecting on the emotions, lessons, and moments that shaped who you are. It's about telling the truth as you lived it, offering insights and inspiration to others. And who knows? Your memoirs could be the centerpiece of someone else's book club discussions.

Whether you find solace in the quiet corners of a library or the bustling energy of a writers' group, both book clubs and writing workshops offer rich opportunities to continue learning and growing. They provide forums for intellectual engagement and building friendships and community connections that enrich your retirement years with stimulating conversations and shared experiences. So go ahead and turn the page to a new chapter in your life, one written just for you, in the company of friends who appreciate a good story as much as you do.

EXPLORING LOCAL MUSEUMS AND CULTURAL SITES

I love the quiet hush of a museum, where every exhibit whispers a story, and every artifact has danced through time to rest before your eyes—what better way to spend an afternoon? Exploring local museums and cultural sites isn't just a leisurely activity; it's an expedition into the heart of human creativity and history. Think of each visit as a mini-adventure, a chance to discover tales of yore, marvel at artistic masterpieces, or unravel the mysteries of science—all within the walls of institutions just a bus ride away.

The cultural enrichment from frequenting local museums is akin to a continuous education that doesn't involve homework or exams. Every exhibit offers a learning opportunity, whether it's understanding the intricacies of ancient civilizations, the bold strokes of modern art, or the groundbreaking discoveries in science and technology. Museums provide a multidimensional learning experience that engages your intellect, senses, and emotions. Picture standing beneath a towering dinosaur skeleton or being enveloped by a panoramic painting that captures a historical battle—you're not just observing; you're experiencing. These moments enrich your understanding of the world and its diverse heritage, making each visit an education and an adventure.

Now, let's talk perks—and not just the kind you get with a good cup of coffee. Membership in a local museum or cultural institution is like holding a golden ticket to a world of exclusive experiences and benefits. Members often enjoy unlimited free admissions, meaning you can visit as frequently as you like, whether for a special exhibit or a peaceful afternoon escape. But that's just the tip of the iceberg. Special events, members-only previews, discounts at gift shops and cafés, and guest passes are typically part of the package. Some memberships also offer reciprocal benefits at other museums nationwide or even globally, which can be a fantastic bonus for those bitten by the travel bug. By becoming a member, you're not just gaining access to art and history; you're becoming part of a community that values and supports cultural preservation and education.

When you visit these treasure troves of culture, don't just passively walk through the exhibits. Engage actively to enrich your experience. Join a guided tour to gain deeper insights and behind-the-scenes stories about the collections. These tours, often led by knowledgeable guides, can provide context unavailable on exhibit labels. Participate in workshops or lectures that many museums offer, ranging from art classes to talks by historians. These programs allow you to delve deeper into specific topics and even try your hand at artistic techniques or scientific experiments. And don't overlook interactive displays—many modern museums have incorporated technology that allows you to interact with exhibits through touch screens, virtual reality, and more, making the learning experience even more dynamic and engaging.

Documenting your visits can enhance your experience exponentially. Whether through photography or journaling, capturing your museum adventures can provide a personal archive of your cultural outings. Photographs can help you remember items that struck an emotional chord and capture details you want to research later. On the other hand, keeping a museum journal allows you to jot down thoughts, impressions, and emotions stirred by the artworks or exhibits. This practice deepens your engagement and creates a beautiful legacy of your cultural explorations that you can reflect on or share with family and friends.

As we wrap up this chapter on lifelong learning beyond the classroom, remember that each museum visit, each documentary watched, and each book club meeting enriches your life with new knowledge and perspectives. These experiences keep your mind active and your curiosity alive, proving that learning doesn't retire when you do. It evolves, offering endless opportunities to explore, understand, and appreciate the world in many forms. So, keep exploring, keep learning, and let each discovery brighten your golden years.

Up next, we'll turn the page from the halls of museums to the great outdoors. Get ready to trade the marble floors for grassy paths as we explore how getting outside can stretch your legs and expand your horizons in the next chapter of our adventure.

ARTS, CRAFTS, AND CREATIVITY

Welcome to the most colorful chapter of your retirement! If you thought your artistic days ended with those finger-painted masterpieces in kindergarten, think again.

Retirement offers a canvas as blank and promising as any you've encountered. It's time to dust off those brushes, uncap those markers or whatever tools tickle your fancy, and dive headfirst into the vibrant world of arts and crafts. Here, mistakes are just unintended brush strokes that often enhance the beauty of your final piece. So, let's channel our inner Picassos and Fridas and explore how the arts can brighten our walls and lives, too.

DISCOVERING YOUR ARTISTIC TALENT IN RETIREMENT

The art world is your oyster, with various mediums to explore. From the velvety strokes of pastels to the bold lines of acrylics, each medium has its personality and secrets to unlock. Watercolors, for instance, can teach you the art of letting go and watching colors blend in ways that are as surprising as life itself. Sculpture, conversely, invites you to get your hands dirty, giving form to your inner visions with clay that molds under your fingertips. Why not dabble a bit in everything? Local craft stores often offer starter kits that allow you to experiment without committing to expensive supplies. You might find that oil paints stir a passion in you that was waiting to burst forth or that charcoal sketches speak to your soul in smudges and shadows. The key is to play, experiment, and let your spirit guide the brush, knife, or chisel.

Now, if you're thinking, "But I'm not an artist," that's precisely where art classes come into play. Many community centers, libraries, and colleges offer courses tailored for beginners and seniors. These classes are less about forging the next gallery star and more about guiding you through the basics while providing a supportive and fun environment. Imagine spending your afternoons surrounded by peers, embarking on their artistic journeys, each canvas telling a story as unique as its creator. Online platforms like Skillshare or Udemy also offer many courses you can enjoy from the comfort of your home. They allow you to pause, rewind, and learn at your pace, which is handy to ensure your cat's portrait captures its regal disdain just right.

Art, in its essence, is about expression. It's a language without words, where colors, shapes, and textures do the talking. Engaging in art can be incredibly therapeutic. It provides a way to process emotions, experiences, and reflections that might be hard to articulate verbally. Studies have shown that engaging in creative activities can significantly reduce stress, anxiety, and even depression. Focusing on a piece of art can serve as a form of meditation, clearing the mind of clutter and creating peace. So, as you paint, sculpt, or draw, think of each stroke as a conversation with yourself, a way to understand and heal parts of you that were perhaps previously tucked away in the shadows.

Your art deserves a special spot—a sanctuary where creativity can bloom unchecked. Setting up a dedicated art space in your home doesn't require an entire studio. A small corner suffused with natural light, a sturdy table, and some organized supplies are all you need to create your atelier. Invest in a few  storage solutions to keep your materials accessible and orderly—think rolling carts with drawers or clear bins. Proper lighting is crucial, especially if your eyesight isn't what it used to be. A combination of natural light and a good task lamp can make all the difference in how you perceive colors and details. Finally, make this space inviting and personal. Maybe hang inspirational quotes on the walls or have a small shelf with art books that inspire you. This nook should call to you, beckoning you to leave the world behind and immerse yourself in the tranquil waters of artistic creation.

As you carve out this space and time for your art, remember that the goal here is joy. Whether your paintings end up on gallery walls or tucked away in your sketchbook, their value lies in the pleasure and fulfillment they bring you. Engaging in art during retirement isn't just about filling time; it's about enriching your life with color, healing, and expression. So, squeeze out some paint and let your soul dance on the canvas. Who knows what masterpieces await the strokes of your brush?

CRAFTING COMMUNITIES: JOINING OR STARTING YOUR OWN

Picture this: A lively group of craft enthusiasts, each with a project in hand, gathered around a large table scattered with bits and pieces of creativity—yarns, fabrics, beads, and more. There's laughter, chatter, and the occasional "ooh" and "aah" over someone's latest creation. You could make this your weekly Tuesday, a time to unwind, learn, and connect. The beauty of crafting isn't just in the finished product but in the process and the company you keep while creating.

Crafting with others brings a bouquet of benefits that solo endeavors might not yield. There's the social perk, of course. Joining a crafting group can plug you into a community of like-minded individuals who share your passion for creating. It's an excellent way to make new friends, especially if you're new to retirement and finding more hours in the day than you know what to do with. These groups often become more than just a place to craft; they evolve into support networks, offering encouragement in your artistic endeavors and life's ups and downs.

Moreover, there's a motivational aspect. We've all been there, enthusiastically starting a project and then watching it collect dust after the initial excitement wanes. A crafting group can keep you accountable, push you to finish what you started, and perhaps inspire you to tackle more ambitious projects.

Finding these crafting sanctuaries can be both an adventure and a delight. Start with local community centers or libraries—they often host or know of existing crafting groups. Craft stores are another goldmine for local crafting circles; they provide supplies and can connect you with others who share your interests. Don't forget about the digital world. Platforms like Meetup.com are fantastic for finding local groups, or if you're more globally minded, sites like Ravelry connect knitters and crocheters worldwide. Facebook groups are another resource, offering many specialty groups where members share projects, tips, and more. Whether you're into quilting, woodwork, or any craft under the sun, there's likely a group waiting for you to join.

Suppose you find that your unique interest isn't represented in the existing groups, or you're itching to lead your own—why not start a crafting group yourself? It's easier than you might think. First, nail down the focus of your group. Will it be general crafting, or will you specialize in pottery or scrapbooking? Once you have your niche, think about logistics. Local community halls, libraries, or even coffee shops often have spaces you can use. Ensure the venue is accessible and has enough room to spread out those crafting supplies. Pick a regular time and day that's convenient for most people. Monthly or biweekly meetings offer a good balance, giving everyone enough time to progress on their projects.

Lastly, encourage a culture of sharing skills and projects within your group. One member could showcase a particular technique or take the lead during a session. Sharing these responsibilities helps less experienced crafters learn and adds a layer of engagement to your meetings. It's about creating a space where everyone feels valued and can contribute regardless of skill level. This approach enriches the group's skill set and strengthens the bonds between members, weaving a tighter community fabric.

Crafting groups are more than just about making things; they're about making connections, sharing skills, and enriching each other's lives through the joy of creating. As you stitch, mold, paint, or knit, you're not just crafting art; you're crafting friendships, weaving a network of support and inspiration that can make all the difference in how richly colored the tapestry of your retirement years becomes.

DIGITAL ART AND PHOTOGRAPHY

Let's turn up the dial on creativity and plunge into the sparkling waters of digital art and photography. It's like painting or shooting with a camera, but you swap out the brushes and darkrooms for a stylus and digital canvases. This exciting world modernizes traditional art forms, opens galaxies of new styles and techniques, and shares opportunities that were once the stuff of science fiction.

Starting with digital art, imagine the freedom of creating without the mess! No more paint on your elbows or chalk dust in your coffee. Digital art requires just a few critical pieces of equipment to begin. A decent computer or tablet and a digital pen or stylus are adequate tools. The software can range from the professional realms of Adobe Photoshop to more user-friendly options like Procreate or Sketchbook, which offer intuitive interfaces perfect for those who might still feel more at home with a physical sketchpad. These programs allow endless undo functions and provide tools that mimic real-world art instruments like watercolors, oils, pastels, and more. The best part? You can experiment without any material costs or cleanup. Change colors, adjust lines, and perfect your masterpiece with a few clicks or taps, all while sitting in your favorite chair.

Now, slide into photography, where the digital revolution has transformed every aspect of capturing, editing, and sharing images. If you're starting, a smartphone might be your best friend. Modern smartphones come equipped with cameras that rival traditional DSLRs in many respects. A DSLR (digital single-lens reflex) camera combines the optics and mechanisms of a single-lens reflex camera with a digital imaging sensor instead of photographic film.

Smartphones are a much simpler but effective option for practicing composition and getting a feel for light and shadow without the intimidation of too many knobs and dials. As you grow more confident, consider stepping up to a DSLR or a mirrorless camera, which offers greater control over every aspect of your image. Play with manual settings like shutter speed, aperture, and ISO to understand a great shot's mechanics. Remember, photography isn't just about pointing and shooting; it's about finding new ways to see the world around you and capturing moments and emotions that speak across time and space.

For those eager to dive deeper, the internet is awash with courses and resources that can turn novices into adept artists and photographers. Platforms like CreativeLive, LinkedIn Learning, and even specific YouTube channels dedicated to digital arts and photography offer tutorials that cover everything from the basics to more advanced techniques. These resources are goldmines of information, often provided by professionals and experts who are skilled in their craft and know how to teach it effectively. They can guide you through complex software tools or tricky photographic techniques you can practice and master at your own pace.

Sharing your creations has never been easier or more rewarding. Platforms like Instagram, DeviantArt, and Behance are perfect for displaying your art and photos to the masses. They connect you with a global network of creatives, and your work might catch the eye of someone on the other side of the planet. However, remember to tread carefully in the digital world. Protect your work by understanding the privacy settings of each platform, and consider watermarking your images to guard against unauthorized use. Engage with other artists and photographers, gather feedback, and participate in communities that continuously inspire and challenge you to refine your craft.

Up next, we delve into the world of writing and publishing, where the power of words opens up new avenues for storytelling and sharing your unique perspectives. Ready your pens and keyboards; it's time to craft stories that resonate and endure.

THE WRITTEN WORD—READING AND WRITING

The written word is like culinary art, but for the brain, instead of sizzling pans and chopping boards, you have pens, keyboards, and that endless buffet of ideas sizzling in your mind. Whether penning down the next great novel or scribbling a heartfelt blog post, writing offers many ways to express, impress, and sometimes dress down your thoughts (politely, of course). So, grab your literary utensils; it's time to cook up some prose that could even make Shakespeare want to peek over your shoulder.

STARTING A BLOG: SHARING YOUR STORIES AND WISDOM

Dipping your toes into the blogging world can feel like finding the perfect coffee shop—there are many out there, but you need the one where your soul feels at home. For us, the retirees and wise world navigators, user-friendly platforms like WordPress, Blogger, and Medium serve up just the right blend of simplicity and functionality. With its plug-and-play features, WordPress lets you customize everything without needing a tech wizard's diploma.

Blogger is Google's offspring, perfect for those who appreciate a straightforward, no-frills approach. Then there's Medium, where the reading audience is built; you just bring your stories to the table. Each platform has its charm, so pick one that feels less like wrestling with technology and more like having a cozy chat over the fence with your neighbor.

Now, about your voice—it's not just about how you speak; it's about what stirs your passion. Finding your voice is like tuning a guitar; it takes tweaking until you hit that sweet note. Start by asking yourself what tickles your fancy. Is it recounting tales from your travel escapades? Sharing wisdom gleaned from decades of career highs and lows? Or perhaps by offering advice on mastering the art of retirement? Whatever it is, let it be something that lights a fire in your belly. Write as if you're sharing stories at a family reunion: passionately, authentically, and often with a touch of humor. Remember, it's not just about broadcasting your thoughts; it's about resonating with your readers, making them nod, laugh, or even tear up.

A blog is not a monologue; it's a dialogue. Engaging with your audience turns passive readers into a vibrant community. Respond to comments with the same enthusiasm you'd show a guest at your dinner party. Use social media not just as a loudspeaker to announce your posts but as a café where conversations happen—share snippets of your life, ask questions, spark discussions, and invite feedback. Platforms like Facebook, Twitter, and Instagram can help amplify your voice, reaching not just friends but also friends of friends and their friends. It's a digital word-of-mouth parade where every share and like can turn your stories into shared experiences.

While we're baring our souls and wisdom online, let's not forget to draw the curtains where needed. The vast and wild internet requires a bit of caution to navigate safely. When blogging, keep personal details like your home address, financial information, or intimate family matters under wraps. Think of it as keeping your valuables safe—not everyone needs to know where you keep your secret chocolate stash, right? Use strong, unique passwords for your blogging accounts, and be wary of scams that often target unsuspecting internet users.

To help solidify your understanding and practical application of these concepts, let's engage in a small exercise. Head to any of the mentioned blogging platforms and create a dummy blog post. Write a brief introduction about a topic you love, explore the platform's interface to customize your post, and familiarize yourself with the settings. This hands-on approach will not only boost your confidence but also spark ideas for your actual blog. Remember, the digital world is your oyster; you're the pearl, so shine on!

As we navigate the labyrinth of literary creation, from blogs to epic memoirs, remember that each word you pen reflects your unique journey through life. Your stories are not just tales; they are beacons of wisdom, laughter, and life lessons, eagerly waiting to be shared on the vast tapestry of human experience. So, let those words flow, and who knows, your blog might be the next go-to spot for inspired readers on a lazy Sunday afternoon or a brisk Monday morning, eager for a slice of your life's pie. Keep writing, keep engaging, and enjoy every moment of this literary feast!

WRITING YOUR LIFE STORY OR MEMOIR

Have you considered writing your autobiography? It's like your life's backstage pass, offering a front-row seat to the highs, the lows, and those miraculous moments when you realized you were out of coffee on a Monday morning. Writing a memoir is not merely jotting down an endless list of "Dear Diary" moments—it's an art form, a way of weaving the threads of your life into a tapestry that captivates and inspires. So, how do you begin such a monumental task? Start with the broad strokes: childhood, young adulthood, major turning points, and the wisdom years. Under each, jot down key events, people, and the emotions they evoked. Don't just write about what happened. Write about how these experiences shaped you, molded your character, and carved your perceptions. Next, start filling in the details. Describe the sights, the sounds, the smells—the burnt toast, the rainy afternoons, the laughter in the hallways. These sensory details breathe life into your words, pulling your readers into the moment.

Now, let's talk about themes and narratives. Every life is a complex narrative, but what are your overarching themes? Resilience, perhaps? Shown through repeated comebacks from life's curve-balls? Or maybe transformation—the journey from timidity to confidence? Identifying these themes isn't just about under-standing your life better; it's about offering your readers a lens through which they can view their own experiences. Themes are the threads that connect disparate events, weaving them into a coherent story that resonates with universal emotions and strug-gles. To unearth these themes, look for patterns in your decisions, turning points, and the values you held dear in different phases of your life. This introspection can illuminate your path and the milestones that mark your journey.

Participation in a writing workshop or group can significantly enrich this process. Imagine a room (or a Zoom call) filled with fellow memoirists, each a guardian of unique life stories. These workshops are gold mines of constructive feedback, emotional support, and creative inspiration. You can test your drafts, receive honest feedback, and refine your narrative here. More than just critique sessions, these groups provide a community—a collective of minds eager to delve into the art of storytelling. They can point out narrative gaps you might have missed, suggest more detailed descriptions, or offer encouragement when the task feels too daunting. Many community colleges, libraries, and online platforms host such groups. Participating in these workshops hones your writing and connects you with a network of writers who understand the joys and challenges of capturing life on paper.

When your manuscript feels ready to leave the nest, it's time to consider publishing options. Today's digital age offers a buffet of publishing paths. For independent spirits, self-publishing is a viable and increasingly popular route. Platforms like Amazon's Kindle Direct Publishing allow you to control every aspect of your book, from the cover design to the pricing. Then there are traditional publishers, where the path is more rigorous but comes with professional editing, marketing, and distribution support. Whichever route you choose, ensure you understand the terms and the process. Research thoroughly, perhaps consult with authors who've walked this path before, and make an informed decision that aligns with your book's goals.

For those looking for guidance through these steps, online resources abound. The website TheMemoirNetwork.com provides tips, courses, and personalized coaching to help you navigate the memoir-writing process from start to finish. Other online resources like Storyworth.com offer a structured way to compile your memories, prompting you with questions and organizing your responses into a coherent narrative.

Several years back, I discovered Storyworth and its capabilities to elicit and compile personal stories. Intrigued, I encouraged my father to use it to chronicle his life's tales. Every week, he received a thought-provoking question from Storyworth, prompting him to reflect on and record his experiences spanning over eight decades. I accessed his responses and engaged in a written dialogue with

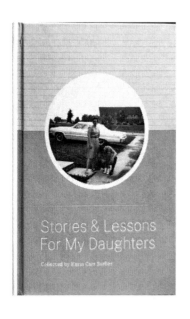

him through the platform. After a year of weekly entries, Storyworth transformed his accumulated stories into a printed hardback book. This process unveiled stories and lessons from my father's life that were previously unknown to me and allowed us to immortalize his memories for future generations. Inspired by the profound impact of this journey, I embarked on my storytelling adventure with Storyworth, eventually crafting a book about my life that I printed and gifted to my daughters the following year.

As you embark on this writing adventure, remember that your life story is not just a series of events; it's a mosaic of experiences, each colored with emotions, decisions, and revelations. Your memoir is a gift—a legacy of wisdom wrapped in the pages of your life's story, ready to be shared with the world. So, set your doubts aside, pick up that pen, power up that laptop, and start writing the chapters only you can write. After all, in the library of human experiences, your book awaits its rightful place.

Up next, we'll explore the enchanting world of gardening and nature, where the beauty of the outdoors enriches our lives and offers a serene escape from the hustle and bustle of daily life.

GARDEN AND NATURE

The great outdoors is beckoning you. Or, for the urban dwellers among us, the great "out-there-somewhere!" While sprawling gardens and vast landscapes might be a rare sight when your view is primarily skyscrapers and concrete, fear not! Urban gardening is here to transform your balcony, windowsill, or even that tiny patch of communal land outside your building into a lush, green oasis. It's time to get your hands dirty—figuratively and literally—and prove that a lack of space is merely an opportunity for creativity. So buckle up your garden belts because we're about to turn every nook and cranny into a flourishing patch of greenery that would make Mother Nature proud!

URBAN GARDENING: GREEN SPACES IN SMALL PLACES

Container Gardening: Cultivating Your Concrete Jungle

Let's start with container gardening, the superhero of the urban gardening world. It's simple and flexible; you can start with just a few pots. Whether it's a tomato plant or a collection of herbs, container gardening allows you to grow an astonishing variety of plants in the most cramped spaces. All you need are containers (think old buckets, wooden crates, or even recycled bottles), some potting soil, seeds or young plants, and a spot that catches a few generous sun rays.

The beauty of container gardening lies in its simplicity and adaptability. You can shuffle the pots around to catch the sun's mood swings, bring them indoors during rogue weather spells, and even theme your garden seasonally—pumpkins for autumn, anyone? Plus, cooking with herbs and veggies that you've grown yourself is profoundly satisfying. Imagine plucking fresh basil right off your windowsill for that pasta sauce simmering on the stove. Magic!

Now, when horizontal space is a luxury, why not think vertically? Vertical gardening is building a living green wall—visually stunning and a fantastic space-saver. You can use trellises, hanging baskets, or even repurpose an old shoe organizer to create your vertical garden. This technique isn't just for small plants; with the proper support, you can grow everything from strawberries to cucumbers.

The trick is to ensure each plant gets enough light and water. Drip irrigation or simple watering can keep your vertical garden thriving. Also, choose plants that naturally grow upwards or can be easily trained to climb. Peas, beans, and certain types of squash love to reach for the sky and will reward your upward thinking with bountiful harvests.

If you're craving more space and soil or want to expand your green endeavors, why not join or start a community garden? These communal spaces are fantastic for growing larger crops and provide an excellent opportunity to connect with neighbors and fellow gardening enthusiasts. Community gardens can transform unused plots into productive green spaces that benefit everyone.

Joining a community garden might involve a small fee or some volunteer hours, but the return is immeasurable. You can access more gardening space, shared tools, and a wealth of collective knowledge. It's like having a library of green thumbs at your disposal! Plus, the sense of community and shared purpose can root you in your neighborhood in new and meaningful ways.

While planning your urban garden, why not choose plants that help our buzzing friends, the pollinators? Bees, butterflies, and other beneficial critters play a crucial role in our ecosystem, allowing plants to reproduce by transporting pollen. Opting for pollinator-friendly plants like lavender, cosmos, and marigolds can turn your garden into a buzzing haven of activity.

Not only will these plants attract beautiful wildlife to your garden, but they'll also help ensure the health of your plants and the local environment. There's nothing like watching a busy bee or a delicate butterfly dance from flower to flower—a small, enchanting reminder of nature's wonders in your urban space.

To get you started on your urban gardening adventure, here's a simple exercise: start a mini herb garden. Herbs like basil, cilantro, and parsley are perfect for containers and don't require much space. Here's what to do:

1. Choose a few containers that fit your space—windowsills and balconies are perfect.
2. Fill them with potting soil.
3. Plant seeds or seedlings of your chosen herbs.
4. Place them in a spot that receives at least six hours of sunlight daily.
5. Water regularly, keeping the soil moist but not waterlogged.

In just a few weeks, you'll have fresh herbs at your fingertips, ready to enhance your culinary creations. This small step can be the gateway to a greener lifestyle and the beginning of your urban gardening journey. So, plant those seeds and watch your concrete surroundings bloom with life and vitality.

BIRDWATCHING: A BEGINNER'S GUIDE

The art of birdwatching is not just about pointing your binoculars at a feathery blur in the distance; it's about unlocking a world where every chirp, flutter, and swoop tells a story. You should reconsider if you're picturing yourself in a camouflage outfit holding an oversized field guide. Modern birdwatching can start right in your backyard or local park with just a few essential tools and a dash of curiosity.

Let's kick off with the essentials—your trusty binoculars. Choosing the right pair can feel a bit like picking out glasses. You want them to enhance your vision without making you look like you're about to embark on a space mission. Look for binoculars labeled with something like "8x42." The "8x" means the bird will appear eight times closer than with your naked eye, and "42" refers to the diameter of the lenses in millimeters, which tells you how much light they let in—a crucial factor for clear, bright views. Once you've got

your binoculars, practice focusing on stationary objects to get a feel for the adjustments. It's like tuning an instrument: a little twist here and a nudge there until the picture is just right.

Now, onto the feathered stars of the show. Identifying birds might seem daunting, but like recognizing faces in a crowd, it gets easier with practice. Start with common birds in your region—your robins, sparrows, and pigeons, the regulars at nature's diner.

Observe their size, colors, and behaviors. A bird pecking the ground has different habits from one that might be darting and diving through the air. Note their songs, too—each bird's call is like a signature tune. You don't need to become a maestro of bird calls, but recognizing a few can make your birdwatching more rewarding.

Transforming your garden into a bird sanctuary is like throwing a housewarming party that says, "Feathered friends, welcome here!" Start with the basics: food, water, and shelter. Plant native shrubs and trees that produce berries, seeds, and nectar—natural bird food sources. These plants provide nourishment, nesting sites, and protection from predators.

Next, consider adding a bird feeder or two. Different feeders attract different guests. Tube feeders are great for small birds like finches and sparrows, while platform feeders will attract a larger crowd, including jays and doves. Don't forget a water source—a simple birdbath can provide drinking and bathing facilities for your avian visitors. Keep it clean and filled, and you'll have birds flocking quickly. Remember, the key to a successful bird-friendly garden is diversity—the more variety in plants and feeders, the wider variety of birds you'll attract.

Birdwatching is more fun with buddies, and joining a local bird-watching group can enhance your experience exponentially. These groups offer guided walks, expert advice, and the camaraderie of fellow bird enthusiasts. It's like joining a book club, but you share notes on nesting habits instead of discussing chapters. Local nature centers, wildlife organizations, and libraries often sponsor birdwatching groups. These outings can be invaluable for beginners, as more experienced birdwatchers can highlight subtle details that might go unnoticed.

In today's digital age, birdwatchers have more tools than ever. Mobile apps like Merlin Bird ID and Audubon Bird Guide are fantastic for beginners. They allow you to enter details about a bird you've seen—the size, color, and what it was doing—and then provide you with a list of possible matches. These apps often include audio files of bird calls, photos, and tips for identification, making them an invaluable pocket guide. My father is an avid bird lover, and when he moved to a new home a few years ago, he wanted to attract cardinals to the backyard. He sat outside with his smartphone and used Merlin Bird ID to play various cardinal calls. The calls were so realistic that a cardinal swooped down and nearly flew into my father's head!

For those who prefer something more tangible, field guides such as *The Sibley Guide to Birds* are classic resources that offer detailed illustrations and information on a wide range of species. Keep a field guide handy in your garden, or take it on birdwatching walks. It's like having a seasoned birdwatcher by your side, ready to impart wisdom on every page.

Birdwatching is more than just a hobby; it's a way to connect with nature, enjoy the outdoors, and even become part of a community of like-minded enthusiasts. Whether gazing through your kitchen window at a feeder or trekking through a local reserve, every bird spotted is a story discovered, a moment of beauty shared with the sky's most graceful inhabitants. So, grab your binoculars and guide, step outside, and let the birdwatching world unfold before your eyes. Who knows what feathered tales await?

NATURE WALKS AND HIKING FOR EVERY LEVEL

Oh, the allure of the untamed wilderness! Whether it's the rustle of leaves underfoot or the distant call of a woodland bird, nature walks and hiking offer a splendid orchestra for the senses. But before you lace up those hiking boots and dash out the door, let's talk trail selection. Not all paths are created equal, especially when your idea of a strenuous workout is reaching for the top shelf of the cookie jar.

Selecting the right trail is like choosing a movie; you want one that fits your mood and physical prowess. Start with local park websites or hiking apps—yes, there's an app for that! These resources often grade trails from easy to challenging, providing details on distance and terrain. For those starting their hiking journey or managing achy joints, look for trails labeled "easy" or "accessible." These are often well-maintained paths with minimal obstacles, ideal for leisurely strolls that won't require a GPS or a rescue team if you wander off track.

For the more adventurous souls who view a bit of sweat as a badge of honor, moderate trails offer a delightful challenge with varied terrain and inclines. These paths promise heart-pumping ascents and rewarding vistas—they are nature's rollercoasters. Just remember, the goal is enjoyment, not exhaustion. Always check trail reviews and chat with park staff or seasoned hikers to understand what lies ahead. It's like scouting movie reviews before committing to two hours of your life you'll never get back.

Why bother traipsing through the woods when you could sip lemonade on your porch? Simple: nature is a miraculous healer. Physically, walking is a low-impact exercise that strengthens your heart, tones your body, and boosts your stamina. It's like a gym but with better views and fresher air.

Mentally, nature walks are a game-changer. Have you ever heard of "forest bathing?" It's not about taking soap to the woods. It's about immersing yourself in the forest atmosphere, and it's scientifically proven to reduce stress, improve mood, and even enhance cognitive function. Each step through nature is a step away from the buzz of technology and the clutter of every day worries. Trees don't care about stock markets or dental appointments; they're too busy being majestic.

Whether you're a solo wanderer or a pack trekker, safety is paramount. Always tell someone your plans— where and when you expect to return. It's like leaving a breadcrumb trail of your whereabouts, minus the actual breadcrumbs.

Pack smart. Water is your best friend; dehydration is not. Snacks are essential, too—think nuts, fruit, energy bars—anything to keep your engine running. And don't forget to wear weather-appropriate gear. A sudden rain can turn a trail into a slippery slide. Layers are essential, as temperatures can swing wildly in nature.

A basic first aid kit, whistle, flashlight, or headlamp should also find space in your backpack. And while we're on the subject, a map and compass might sound old school, but GPS signals can be unreliable in the woods. Old school doesn't mean outdated—it means tried and true.

While walking is excellent, engaging with your surroundings enriches the experience. Try your hand at nature photography or sketching. These activities force you to look, to notice the curve of a leaf, the pattern of bark, or the play of light through the trees.

Foraging can also add an element of treasure hunting to your hikes. Learning to safely identify and harvest wild edibles like berries or mushrooms is like unlocking nature's pantry. Ensure you're foraging responsibly and legally—nature's pantry isn't an all-you-can-eat buffet.

As you wander through the woods, over hills, and along streams, remember that each step into nature is more than just physical exercise; it's a step into a world of beauty, peace, and discovery. Let the birds serenade you, the wind dance with you, and the paths inspire you. And as this chapter closes, remember that the trails you walk in nature are not just dirt paths; they are journeys into the heart of the world itself.

In wrapping up our stroll through "Garden and Nature," we've unearthed the joys of urban gardening, the thrill of birdwatching, and the soul-soothing magic of nature walks. Each step and seed sown is a testament to the natural world's enduring allure and restorative power. As we close this chapter, let's carry forward the peace found in chirping birds, rustling leaves, and quiet paths into bustling everyday life. Up next, we turn our attention to the world of volunteering, where giving a bit of yourself to the world returns a wealth of joy and connection. Let's step forward, ready to plant seeds of kindness and community as we continue exploring the fruitful adventures of retirement.

VOLUNTEERING AND PHILANTHROPY

Volunteering—the noble art of giving without expecting a receipt. It's like investing in stocks, except the dividends are smiles, a thank-you, and that warm, fuzzy feeling of making the world a tad brighter. Volunteering might seem daunting, but fear not! Whether your passion lies in cuddling cats at an animal shelter or swinging hammers at a Habitat for Humanity building, there's a place for every willing heart. Let's roll up our sleeves, put on our philanthropic thinking caps, and find that perfect volunteer match that makes your soul sing (off-key is perfectly fine).

FINDING THE RIGHT VOLUNTEER OPPORTUNITY

First things first: What tickles your fancy? Volunteering isn't just about what you are good at; it's also about what lights up your LED sneakers. Start by jotting down your hobbies, skills, and passion projects. Are you a wizard with woodworking tools? Do strays tend to follow you home because they sense a fellow animal lover? Or do you have a green thumb that could turn a desert into an oasis? These interests are clues to finding a volunteer role that feels less like a chore and more like a personal party.

Now, consider how these passions align with potential volunteering opportunities. Love books? Libraries or literacy programs could use your enthusiasm. Is cooking your way of spreading love? Soup kitchens or Meals on Wheels programs are calling your name. The key is to match your joy with the needs of organizations—creating a win-win situation where time flies, and you occasionally wonder who's helping whom here.

Once you've pinpointed your interests, it's time to play detective and scope out organizations that could use a hero like you. Start local. Community boards, town websites, and local newspapers are treasure troves of volunteer needs. But don't stop there—expand your horizon with a sprinkle of technology. Websites like VolunteerMatch.org and Idealist.org can match your interests with nonprofit organizations you may be interested in.

When researching, look deeply into the mission statement and check out what current volunteers say. Sites like GreatNonprofits.org offer reviews and testimonials that can give you the real scoop on the organization's environment. Is it supportive? Is it effective? Does it make volunteers wear neon tutus? (Hey, you never know!)

Consider using a volunteer matching service for those who feel overwhelmed by the buffet of choices. Volunteermatch.org is one such site. Think of it as a personal shopping assistant but for your philanthropic wardrobe. These services take your interests, skills, and availability and match you with organizations that fit your unique profile. These platforms aren't just about convenience; they're about customization and ensuring your volunteer time is spent wisely and joyfully. These services often offer trial opportunities, allowing you to dip your toes before diving in. It's like a "try before you buy" offer with a social impact.

Speaking of trying, the world of volunteering is flexible. Think of it as a buffet. Sample a bit of this, a tad of that. Help at an event here, assist in an office there. Each experience provides insight into the organization's culture, the impact of your work, and whether you want to turn this volunteer fling into a long-term commitment.

When you find that perfect fit, where the work speaks to your heart and your efforts are met with appreciation, consider deepening your involvement. Take on a leadership role or initiate a project. Leadership is your chance to attend the party and throw it. And remember, commitment isn't about chaining yourself to a cause; it's about choosing to stand by it because it adds a chapter of meaning and joy to your life story.

STARTING A CHARITY INITIATIVE

When the itch to do good turns into a burning desire to start something new, it's time to consider launching a charity initiative. It's akin to nurturing a garden, but you're cultivating impact and change instead of flowers. The first step? Identify a glaring need in your community. Whether it's a lack of arts programs for youth or insufficient support for older people, the key is to find a gap that resonates with your passion and your community's needs. Walk around your neighborhood, talk to locals, attend community meetings, and you might stumble upon an issue that tugs at your heartstrings and screams for attention.

Once you've pinpointed this need, the fun begins with planning and organization. Imagine you're plotting a treasure hunt, where the treasure is the successful launch of your initiative. Start with a clear mission statement—this is your map. It should outline what your charity aims to achieve and why. Next, sketch out a strategic plan, like you're crafting a recipe for a spectacular cake. What ingredients will you need? These are your resources, like funds, materials, and human capital. What steps are required to mix these ingredients into a successful outcome? These might include fundraising events, awareness campaigns, and partnership development. Remember, the more detailed your plan, the smoother the execution.

No captain sails a ship alone, and you'll need a crew. Building a team is about finding individuals whose skills complement each other, like spices in a stew. Look for people who share your vision and bring essential skills, such as marketing prowess, financial skills, or a knack for inspiring volunteers. Use your networks, social media, and community bulletins to reach potential team members. Host informal meet-ups to gauge compatibility and commitment. Think of it as assembling a band where the harmony of skills and personalities can make beautiful music or, in this case, impactful social change.

Lastly, let's discuss the nuts and bolts—legal and financial considerations. Navigating this maze can be tricky, but it's crucial for ensuring your charity stands on solid ground. Start by registering your initiative as a nonprofit; this can help with tax exemptions and legality. Understand the financial regulations that govern fundraising and charity operations in your area. Keeping meticulous records from the start can save you some headaches later. Consider consulting with a legal expert specializing in nonprofit law to dot the i's and cross the t's. This step ensures that your good intentions are backed by good practices, keeping your charity's doors open and your mission thriving.

John's journey to founding a local charity, Blessings in Disguise, began with personal hardship. After losing his life savings to a fraudulent investment firm, he faced severe financial distress, losing his home and car amid an economic down-turn. Despite these challenges, the support from friends and family inspired him with a profound sense of gratitude. He promised to pay

this kindness forward by assisting others in similar situations when he got back on his feet. To fulfill this promise, John estab-lished a 501c3 charity to aid Ohio residents facing short-term disability, unemployment, or long-term illness. Initially focused on providing immediate support, the charity later expanded its services to assist seniors in acquiring necessary appliances not covered or quickly supplied by Medicare. Over a decade later, the organization has touched the lives of over 10,000 individuals, sustained by a dedicated board of directors and a team of volun-teers. You never know the extent of the ripple effect your act of kindness, through initiating a charity, can have on your community.

Initiating a charity requires grit, passion, and a sprinkle of audac-ity. It's about seeing a need and deciding you're the right person to do something about it. With careful planning, a dedicated team, and a clear legal understanding, you can turn a spark of an idea into a beacon of hope and change. Now, let's roll up those sleeves and turn that passion into action!

MENTORING THE NEXT GENERATION

Imagine yourself as a seasoned ship captain, navigating not just the seas but also guiding the bright-eyed deckhands eager to learn the ropes. That's what mentoring feels like. It's a chance to pass on your treasure trove of knowledge and experiences to eager minds, helping them learn to steer their own ships someday. Mentoring isn't just about teaching; it's a give-and-take relationship that benefits both the mentor and the mentee. It's like having a coffee chat where you leave the table richer than when you sat down.

The beauty of mentoring lies in its dual benefits. For mentees, having a mentor is like having a GPS in the often-confusing career and personal development journey. Mentors provide guidance, encouragement, and insight to help navigate challenges and recognize opportunities. For mentors, the process is equally rewarding. Sharing your knowledge helps solidify your understanding and often provides new perspectives on familiar issues. Moreover, the satisfaction of helping someone else grow and succeed is a reward in itself, much like watching a plant you've nurtured bloom spectacularly.

Finding the right mentoring opportunities can sometimes feel like finding a needle in a haystack. However, with the right tools and persistence, you can find opportunities that align with your expertise and interests. Start with professional associations or alumni networks; these organizations often have formal mentoring programs for experienced professionals eager to give back. Online platforms like LinkedIn also facilitate mentoring connections. For instance, its Career Advice Hub matches users with potential mentors or mentees within their professional networks.

To be an effective mentor, remember a few best practices. First, clear communication is critical. Be open about your expectations, and encourage your mentee to do the same. I always let the mentee know that it is their responsibility to set the meeting agendas to ensure we focus on the areas most applicable to them. This communication will help establish a relationship based on mutual respect and understanding. Setting specific goals can also keep the mentoring relationship focused and productive. Whether improving a skill, learning a new technology, or developing leadership abilities, having clear goals gives both parties a sense of direction.

Moreover, effective mentoring involves more listening than talking. The aim is to guide, not dictate. By listening attentively, you can better understand your mentee's challenges and aspirations and provide tailored advice that resonates with their unique circumstances. Remember, mentoring is not about creating a mini-version of yourself but helping mentees become their best version.

Sharing personal stories and experiences can significantly enhance the mentoring experience. Your stories make the guidance more relatable and help mentees see practical examples of how challenges can be navigated successfully and opportunities seized. When you share your failures and successes, you humanize yourself, making it easier for the mentee to connect with you and learn from your experiences.

As this chapter on mentoring closes, remember that the essence of mentoring is the joy of giving and receiving knowledge. It's about building bridges between generations, transferring wisdom, and fostering growth. Each mentoring relationship is a thread in the larger fabric of our professional and personal communities, strengthening connections and enriching lives. As we turn the page from fostering individual growth to embracing community-wide initiatives in the next chapter, let's carry forward the spirit of mentorship, recognizing that our shared knowledge and experiences are the most valuable legacy we can pass on.

VOLUNTEER BOARD OPPORTUNITIES

Annually, countless individuals offer their skills and knowledge to impact nonprofit organizations positively by joining their boards. Serving as a board member is not just about providing essential intellectual and strategic support; it's about strengthening the very fabric of our communities and backing causes close to our hearts.

Engaging in nonprofit board service is a remarkable avenue for personal growth and professional development. It offers a unique chance to enhance leadership abilities, widen networks with peers, professionals, and community figures, and foster meaningful connections for future opportunities. Board service is a path with chances for learning, influence, and mentorship. To aid in assessing whether board service aligns with your aspirations and how to embark on this enriching journey, BoardSource.com offers tailored learning experiences designed to guide you. Take the board service readiness quiz to explore options that fit your interests and passions and see if volunteer board opportunities will work for you.

ENTREPRENEURSHIP AND PART-TIME WORK

The sweet sound of the cash register or the ping of a payment notification on your phone can be like a song to your ears. Retirement might mean you've hung up your nine-to-five boots, but who says you can't lace up a different pair for a little entrepreneurial jig? Think of this phase as your new playground where the slide is steeper, but boy, the ride is exhilarating. Whether you're looking to turn your quilt-making passion into a crafty business or keep your mind sharp with freelancing, let's dive into the financial nitty-gritty that keeps the engines running without derailing the fun.

FINANCIAL CONSIDERATIONS

Now, before you set up your lemonade stand (adult version, of course, perhaps with a splash of something stronger), let's talk business—or, in this case, dollars. Navigating financial waters in retirement, especially when drawing Social Security or other government assistance, is like playing Monopoly. However, in this case, the rules aren't printed inside the box lid.

First off, if you're receiving Social Security benefits, diving into part-time work or starting a business could affect how much you pocket from Uncle Sam each month. Why? Because there's a limit to how much you can earn before your benefits shrink. But don't let this put a damper on your entrepreneurial parade! Wages earned while on Social Security can help increase your Social Security benefit amount. Planning is your best friend here. Consider consulting with a financial advisor who understands the ins and outs of Social Security implications. They can help you strategize, maximizing your earnings while keeping your benefits as plump as possible.

Also, if you're benefiting from Medicaid or other income-based government assistance, earning additional income might require you to sing a new tune regarding eligibility.

Each state has its own orchestra playing a slightly different medley regarding these rules, so visiting your local benefits office or chatting with a financial maestro who knows how to conduct a deep dive into these regulations is worthwhile.

TURNING HOBBIES INTO A BUSINESS

Imagine turning your passion for patchwork quilts or your knack for knitting whimsical woolen scarves into more than just a hobby. Yes, it's time to consider putting a price tag on those creations and sharing them with the world—or at least with anyone who appreciates a cozy, handmade scarf. But before you start dreaming of your crafts adorning boutique shelves, let's talk about evaluating the market potential. It's like figuring out if there's enough love for lasagna before opening a pasta shop.

First, dip your toes into the market waters to see if they're warm. Start by checking out local craft fairs and online marketplaces.

Notice what's selling and what stalls are attracting the biggest crowds. Is there a buzz around handcrafted jewelry, or are custom paintings the belle of the ball? This reconnaissance mission can reveal much about consumer tastes and trends. You could also float a few of your creations on platforms like Etsy or eBay to gauge interest. Think of it as a sneak preview for your potential audience—do they applaud with their wallets?

Let's get down to brass tacks with some essential business planning. If the thought of business plans sends shivers down your spine, think of it as planning an epic road trip. You wouldn't just jump in the car and hope to find the Grand Canyon eventually, right? Your business plan is your roadmap. It outlines your destination (business goals), how you plan to get there (strategies), and what you'll need for the journey (resources). Start with a simple outline: What are you selling? Who are your customers? How will you reach them? And crucially, how will you make money? This plan will evolve, but without it, you're driving blind.

As you sketch your business blueprint, consider your financial landscape, marketing avenues, and operational details. Financial planning isn't just about counting pennies; it's about forecasting expenses, pricing your products, and setting a budget that allows you to grow sustainably. Marketing, on the other hand, is how you shout from the rooftops about your unique products. In today's digital age, online platforms and social media are not just tools; they are lifelines to your customers. Create vibrant, engaging content that tells your brand's story. Show behind-the-scenes peeks of your creative process or happy customers with their purchases. It's about creating connections, not just trans-actions.

Speaking of online prowess, let's not forget the power of social media and online platforms. They are your stage, and your products are the show's stars. Platforms like Instagram, Pinterest, and Facebook are ideal for selling products, offering a direct line to visually oriented customers. Use these platforms to showcase your products, interact with your followers, gather feedback, and drive trends. The key is consistency and engagement. Regular posts, interactive content, and responsive communication can turn followers into fans and customers.

Before you get too caught up in the excitement, remember there are legal tunes to play. Registering your business might not be as thrilling as making sales, but it's just as essential. Depending on where you live, this might mean obtaining a business license, registering for sales tax, or even trademarking your brand. And let's not forget about copyright, especially if your creations are as original as Picasso's. Legally protecting your business can prevent others from profiting from your passion. Think of it as building a fence around your vegetable garden to keep the rabbits out—it's about safeguarding what you've worked hard to grow.

Navigating these legal waters might require professional advice. Consulting with a lawyer specializing in small businesses can provide clarity and direction, ensuring your business starts on the right foot and continues to stride confidently forward. Whether understanding the nuances of copyright law or navigating the complexities of business registration, professional counsel can prevent legal pitfalls that might trip up your business later on.

So, as you consider turning your hobby into a business, remember that it's about more than just making money—it's about sharing your passion with the world, learning new skills, and even challenging yourself in ways you never expected. From market research and business planning to mastering social media and navigating legal requirements, each step is a building block in constructing a business that reflects both your craft and character.

CONSULTING AND FREELANCING IN RETIREMENT

Retirement: that time when you can finally kick back, relax, and … start consulting? Absolutely! Your years of hard-earned expertise don't need to retire when you do. Consulting or freelancing in your golden years isn't just about keeping the lights on—it's about keeping the brain cells firing, the network buzzing, and maybe even padding the wallet. Think of it as your encore career; you're back by popular demand!

Let's zero in on leveraging that professional expertise first. Here you are, with decades of experience. This knowledge is the foundation of your consulting or freelancing venture. Your industry experience is a gold mine, and it's high time to stake your claim. Whether it's marketing, engineering, education, or any other field, your insights and skills are incredibly valuable, especially to those just starting careers or companies needing a seasoned eye. Begin by outlining the services you can offer. Can you provide strategic advice, hands-on training, project management, or specialized services like copywriting or graphic design? Pin down what you excel at and enjoy doing, then prepare to put that expertise to work.

Finding freelance opportunities might sound daunting, but it's much like dating—finding the right match is vital, as there are plenty of fish in the sea. Start with your professional network. Reach out to former colleagues, employers, and industry contacts. Let them know you're available for freelance or consulting gigs. Personal referrals can open doors that online applications cannot.

Next, harness the power of the internet. Platforms like LinkedIn, Upwork, and Freelancer are not just digital spaces but bustling marketplaces teeming with opportunities. Create a compelling profile showcasing your skills and past projects, and start connecting with potential clients. Remember, each connection is a possible lead. Treat these platforms as ongoing networking events with less small talk and more direct opportunities.

Setting up as a freelancer involves more than just printing business cards and launching a website (though those are definitely on the checklist). You've got to think about the nuts and bolts, like how you'll structure your business (Sole proprietorship? LLC?), manage your finances, and the inevitable taxes. Getting the administrative ducks in a row isn't the most thrilling part of freelancing, but it's crucial. Consider consulting an accountant or using online accounting software designed for freelancers to help manage invoices, expenses, and tax submissions. As for setting rates, that's an art in and of itself. Research standard rates in your industry, but also evaluate the value you bring to the table. Your rates should reflect your expertise and specific service, balanced against market expectations.

Maintaining a work-life balance as a freelancer or consultant might be the trickiest part of this gig. Without the structure of a nine-to-five job, work can spill over into personal time, turning what should be a flexible schedule into a 24/7 grind. Set clear boundaries from the start—decide on work hours, communicate your availability to clients, and be disciplined about logging off. You can take a mid-week golf break or lunch with friends, but keep the deadlines sacred. The beauty of freelancing during retirement is that you write the rules. Maybe you work best in the early mornings or late at night. You may prefer intensive workdays followed by free days. Find the rhythm that suits your lifestyle and stick to it, ensuring you have ample time to enjoy the retirement perks you've earned.

As you navigate the exciting world of freelancing or consulting, remember that this is your chance to redefine your professional life on your terms. You bring a wealth of knowledge and experience in high demand, and now you can share it on your schedule and at your pace.

THE JOY OF SEASONAL EMPLOYMENT

Imagine the possibility of working with the rhythmic changes of the seasons—embracing the hustle and bustle of a holiday retail rush in winter, guiding thrilled tourists under the warm summer sun, or maybe stepping into a Halloween pop-up store that needs your flair for spooky creativity. Seasonal employment isn't just about earning extra cash; it's about infusing variety into your life with commitments with an expiration date just long enough to stay exciting but short enough to keep from becoming mundane.

The spectrum of opportunities in seasonal employment is as broad as your imagination. Retail giants often beef up their staff for the winter holidays, amusement parks swell their ranks in the summer, ski resorts are looking for help in the winter months, and tax season can mean firms are looking for temporary help. Each of these roles comes with its own set of experiences and learning opportunities. Imagine guiding a group of eager tourists around the local landmarks and sharing stories you love or helping shoppers choose the perfect gift that could make someone's holiday special. The roles are as varied as the seasons themselves, ensuring there is likely something that resonates with your interests and schedule.

Now, let's chat about the perks. Seasonal work often comes with a side of flexibility that is as refreshing as a cool autumn breeze. These jobs can fit like puzzle pieces into the gaps of your daily life, allowing you to work when it suits you best. Many retirees find this flexibility ideal for balancing leisure  and family time with a bit of structured activity. Besides putting some extra green in your wallet, seasonal jobs offer a unique platform for social interaction. They pull you into dynamic environments where you can meet new people, engage in lively conversations, and make a few new friends. This social spice often reinvigorates one's daily routine, making life seem more vibrant.

Hunting down these seasonal gigs can be as simple as keeping your eyes peeled for "Help Wanted" signs in local store windows or as modern as navigating online job portals like Indeed or Monster. Timing is crucial; start your search a few months before the season begins to secure the best positions. Local newspapers, community bulletin boards, and employment websites often start advertising these opportunities well in advance. Don't shy away from visiting local employment agencies either—they can offer personalized assistance and alert you to opportunities you might not find on your own.

Transitioning to seasonal work from a full-time career or other retirement activities is like switching dance partners mid-song. It requires a bit of adjustment to the new tempo.

Start slow; take on a part-time seasonal job to gauge how well you juggle the latest schedule with your current lifestyle. This approach helps ease the transition, allowing you to enjoy the best of both worlds without feeling overwhelmed. Remember, the beauty of seasonal work lies in its temporary nature, giving you the freedom to step back after the season and reflect on your experiences before committing to the next opportunity.

In wrapping up, seasonal employment offers a refreshing mixture of flexibility, social interaction, and the joy of something new at regular intervals, perfect for keeping retirement lively and engaging. As we close this chapter on entrepreneurship and part-time work, remember that stepping into these opportunities is not just about staying busy—it's about continuing to grow, learn, and interact in ways that enrich your life. As the seasons change, so too might your interests or needs, leading us into our next exploration: community and legacy, where we delve into how your contributions can weave into the larger tapestry of community life.

COMMUNITY AND LEGACY

Roll up your sleeves and put on your party hat because it's time to dive into the exhilarating world of organizing local events and festivals! Picture this: Children's laughter as they dart between stands, the murmur of excited chatter, the tantalizing aroma of street food filling the air. Whether it's a quaint book fair, a lively music festival, or an avant-garde art show, pulling off a successful community event can be as rewarding as it is challenging. So, let's break down the brass tacks of turning your grand idea into a grand day out for everyone.

ORGANIZING LOCAL EVENTS AND FESTIVALS

First things first: Every event starts with a spark—an idea. But just like a spark can either fizz out or ignite a bonfire, the success of your event hinges on how well you fan that initial flame. Begin by setting clear, achievable goals. What do you want to accomplish? Is it fundraising, community building, or simply providing entertainment? Once your goals are clear, sketch out the framework.

Decide on the venue, date, and theme. Consider this phase as setting up a stage—every detail adds to the drama.

Now, no event can run smoothly without a crew, and that's where building a stellar volunteer team comes into play. Volunteers are the unsung heroes behind the scenes—the oil that keeps the engine running. Recruiting them, however, requires a mix of charm and strategy. Start by identifying the volunteer roles you need—ticket sellers, security, set-up crews, or perhaps face painters for the kids. Reach out through social media, local community boards, and volunteer websites. Remember, people are more willing to lend a hand if they feel they're part of something exciting. Keep your calls for volunteers enthusiastic and specific, and always acknowledge their contributions. A little appreciation goes a long way in keeping spirits high and turnover low.

Promoting your event is next on the agenda. In today's digital age, an effective promotion strategy is more than just plastering posters on community bulletin boards. Harness the power of social media platforms to create a buzz. Craft posts that capture the essence of your event with vibrant images and engaging content. Use targeted ads to reach your desired audience, and don't shy away from partnering with local influencers or community figures who can amplify your message. Email newsletters are another arrow in your quiver; they can keep your community informed and engaged as the event day approaches. Remember, the key to effective promotion is consistent communication—keep your audience in the loop, and they'll likely mark their calendars.

Finally, after the last guest has left and the lights are turned off, it's time to reflect on the event's success. Evaluating what went well and what didn't is crucial for learning and improvement. Gather feedback from attendees, volunteers, and vendors. What did they enjoy the most? What could be improved? Use surveys or informal chats to collect these insights. Also, review your objectives—did you meet your fundraising goal? Did the community turn out as expected? This post-event analysis is like looking through a rearview mirror; it helps you understand the journey you've just completed and guides your planning for future events.

Organizing local events and festivals is no small feat, but with proper planning, a dedicated team, and effective promotion, it can be an incredibly enriching experience. It's more than just logistics; it's about weaving your community's diverse threads together to create a tapestry of shared experiences and memories. So, grab your planner and phone, and start bringing people together—one spectacular event at a time.

LIFE LESSONS: SHARING YOUR KNOWLEDGE WITH SCHOOLS AND COMMUNITY CENTERS

Imagine stepping into a classroom not as a student but as a beacon of wisdom, a treasure trove of life lessons waiting to be shared. Retirement opens up a spectacular stage where the spotlight isn't on your age but on the rich experiences you bring. Schools and community centers often seek individuals who can offer more than just textbook knowledge—they seek a real-world experience that breathes life into their curriculum and activities. This is where you, with decades of expertise and a suitcase full of stories, come into play.

Educational volunteering is about turning your past into a pathway for others. Consider the subjects that ignite your passion —history, science, art, or even basic financial literacy—and imagine imparting that knowledge to eager young minds. Many educational settings cherish the involvement of seasoned adults because you bring context to the content. For instance, discussing World War II is profoundly different when you can share personal

family stories or artifacts. It's about making history leap off the page or showing how mathematical principles are not just theories but foundations that support bridges, technology, and economies.

Now, let's talk about setting up workshops or seminars. These aren't your run-of-the-mill lectures. Picture more of a collaborative space where ideas bounce like ping-pong balls, and curiosity isn't just welcomed; it's served with a cup of tea and a biscuit. Your role?

You're the orchestra conductor who makes sure every instrument is heard. Start by choosing a topic close to your heart and relevant to your audience. It could be as straightforward as "The Art of Everyday Photography" or as intricate as "Understanding Blockchain Technology." The key is in your preparation. Gather materials, think through your presentation, and, perhaps most importantly, be ready to learn yourself. Yes, even as you teach, be open to the new perspectives and insights your audience will bring.

Collaboration with educational institutions doesn't just amplify your impact—it multiplies it. By partnering with schools, colleges, and community centers, you can help develop programs that leverage your expertise. These partnerships might involve more formal teaching or creating extracurricular activities that complement the academic curriculum. For example, if you're a retired engineer, you might help set up a robotics club that gives students practical experience while igniting their interest in STEM fields. These collaborations can also lead to opportunities for other retirees to contribute, creating a community of educators who are not bound by age but driven by a desire to enrich the educational landscape.

In these settings, your age is an asset, your experience a gift, and your willingness to engage a pathway to enriching not just the minds of others but also your own life. As you step into class-rooms or community centers, you're not just sharing knowledge but shaping futures and continuing a lifelong journey of learning and connection. So, grab your wealth of knowledge and step into these educational arenas where every lesson you teach also teaches you, and every life you touch also transforms yours.

WRITING AND PUBLISHING GUIDEBOOKS

Have you ever considered that your wealth of knowledge and experience could fill the pages of a book? Not just any book, but a guidebook that could light the way for others walking paths you've already tread. Whether it's mastering the art of French cooking, navigating the complexities of woodworking, or recounting your travels to hidden corners of the globe, your expertise is a treasure trove awaiting discovery by eager learners. Picture this: Your name on a book cover, your wisdom passed down through pages, your legacy inked in the annals of libraries and bookshelves. Let's unfold how you can transform your know-how into a guidebook that informs and inspires.

First, gathering your knowledge into a structured format is like assembling a jigsaw puzzle where each piece is a nugget of wisdom you've collected over the years. Start by outlining the chapters based on themes or lessons you want to share. Dig through your old journals and photo albums, or pick the brains of peers who share your passion. Organize these insights in a way that builds upon each other, creating a narrative that guides the reader from novice to knowledgeable. Remember, the most engaging guidebooks reflect a genuine voice and passion, so let your personality shine through your writing. Share anecdotes and personal stories that vividly depict your experiences, making the guidebook informative, deeply personal, and engaging. My first published book was a guide-book for beginners wanting to travel to Africa. I researched, gath-ered my photos, and reflected on my six trips to Africa. I completed and published a short, easy-to-read book in about one month. Yes, you can do it too!

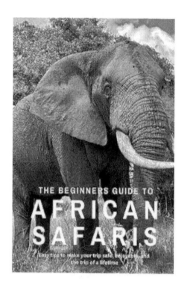

So, let's talk about the magic wand of modern publishing: self-publishing platforms. Gone are the days when landing a publisher was as challenging as climbing Everest. Platforms like Amazon's Kindle Direct Publishing, Smashwords, or Blurb have democra-tized the publishing world, allowing you to publish without the need for literary agents or publishing houses. These platforms offer tools that walk you through the publishing process from start to finish, including formatting your book, designing the cover, and setting up distribution channels. They often provide resources on how to price your book and even market it globally. The beauty of self-publishing is its control. You decide how your book looks, how it is priced, and how it is sold.

Regarding marketing, navigating this realm effectively turns your guidebook from a personal project into a public resource. Start by identifying your target audience. Who would benefit most from your book? Is it DIY enthusiasts, cooking hobbyists, or travel aficionados? Understanding your audience helps tailor your marketing strategies to channels where these readers will likely spend their time. Create a buzz by leveraging social media platforms, starting a blog, or hosting webinars and workshops on topics related to your guidebook. Engaging content that gives potential readers a taste of what to expect from your book can pique their interest and lead to sales. Additionally, consider reaching out to influencers or thought leaders in your book's genre who might be willing to endorse your guidebook or offer a foreword.

Lastly, consider the legacy your guidebook leaves. Writing a book isn't just about sales numbers or topping bestseller lists; it's about imprinting your mark on the world and sharing valuable knowledge that can empower others. Your book could help someone develop a new hobby, discover a passion, or even change their career path. It's about creating something that lasts longer than you—a source of inspiration and guidance for future generations.

By turning your expertise into a guidebook, you're leaving a legacy and embarking on a rewarding adventure that celebrates your life's work. So, grab your pen, power up your laptop, and start drafting the first chapter of what could be the most fulfilling project of your life. Who knows—your guidebook might just become the manual someone else has been searching for, the guide that lights the way on their journey of discovery.

CRAFTING AND DONATING HANDMADE GOODS

Picture this: Your cozy living room transformed into a mini-factory of goodwill, where every stitch and purl you knit infuses the world with warmth and care. Yes, dear reader, we're diving into the heartwarming realm of crafting handmade goods for charity—where your crafting skills can wrap a cold stranger in a warm blanket or cap a needy head with a snug beanie. It's about turning your hobby into a beacon of hope and stitching together a legacy of kindness, one woven item at a time.

Now, let's roll up our sleeves and unravel the yarn of how to start. Crafting for charity isn't just about what you make but also the purpose behind it. Begin by selecting projects that resonate with you deeply. Knitting tiny hats for premature babies may tug at your heartstrings, or sewing quilts for veterans may wrap your soul in gratitude. Whatever you choose, let your passion lead your projects. This personal connection adds a layer of love to your creations and keeps your motivation bustling through each loop and stitch.

Organizing a crafting group for charity can magnify your impact and spin your solo project into a community tapestry of giving. Start by gathering a group of like-minded crafters—friends, community members, or even online acquaintances—who share your passion for crafting and charity. Meet regularly in person at a local community center or via video chats. These crafting sessions can become a cherished space for sharing techniques, swapping patterns, and sharing many laughs. The key here is consistency; regular meetings keep the momentum going and ensure that your charitable goals are met stitch by stitch.

Finding recipients for your crafted goods adds another layer of meaning to your work. Contact local charities, hospitals, skilled nursing facilities, and shelters to understand their needs. Many organizations constantly need items like blankets, scarves, or mittens, especially during the colder months. Be sure to ask about any specific requirements they might have, such as sizes, materials, or patterns, to ensure that your creations meet their needs and standards. This step is crucial—it ensures that your effort truly benefits the recipients and meets a real need rather than just filling a closet.

The impact of donating handmade goods stretches beyond the tangible warmth of a knitted blanket or the snug fit of a crocheted hat. Each item carries a story of care, a personal touch that commercial items cannot replicate. Recipients often feel a profound sense of being cared for, a feeling that someone took the time and effort to create something just for them. This personal connection can be compelling, especially for those going through tough times. For the crafters, creating and giving handmade goods provides a deep sense of fulfillment and connection to the community. It's a beautiful cycle of giving that nourishes both the giver and the receiver.

Crafting for charity weaves together threads of creativity, community, and compassion to create a fabric of goodwill that blankets those in need with warmth and wraps the crafters with a sense of purpose. It's about more than just yarn and fabric—it is weaving love into every fiber of your community, creating connections that warm hearts and heal spirits.

ENGAGING WITH LOCAL POLITICS AND ADVOCACY GROUPS

Step right up to the civic engagement buffet, where the choices are as varied as the potential impact you can have on your community. Imagine wielding the power to influence local policies, champion causes you're passionate about, and even steer the community toward a brighter, more inclusive future. Yes, it's time to talk politics, but not the kind that has you switching off the TV. We're diving into the grassroots kind, where every little action counts and every voice can echo through the halls of local governance.

Dipping your toes into the local political scene might sound as daunting as singing solo at a community concert, but fear not! It's all about starting small. Attend a town hall meeting, or better yet, become a regular fixture there. These meetings are the behind-the-scenes of decisions in your town or city. They are where you can raise your hand, voice an opinion, or immerse yourself in local issues. It's like being in the audience of your favorite live show, except you might get a chance to direct an episode or two. And if you're feeling courageous, why not run for a local board or committee position? It's a direct line to the decision-making process, and hey, it is more exhilarating than your morning cross-word puzzle.

If diving headfirst into politics makes you nervous, why not ease in by joining an advocacy group? These are the clubs where passion meets action. Whether you are interested in environmental conservation, passionate about education reform, or eager to tackle senior citizen rights, a group in your community will likely champion these causes. Joining an advocacy group connects you with like-minded individuals looking to make a difference. It's not just about holding signs or chanting at rallies; it's about strategizing, educating, and, sometimes, navigating the nitty-gritty of legislative frameworks. Think of it as joining a book club, but instead of discussing the latest mystery novel, you're plotting a real-world impact campaign.

Engaging in grassroots campaigning is boots-on-the-ground work, where you and your fellow group members might canvas neighborhoods, phone banks, or organize community events to rally support for your cause. It's about putting a face to the name of change. Campaigning teaches you the art of persuasion, the thrill of a well-organized event, and the satisfaction of seeing your efforts materialize into tangible outcomes. Plus, the skills you pick up—public speaking, organizing, networking—are like badges of honor you get to wear long after the campaign signs disappear.

But let's remember the real meat of the matter: making a difference. Your involvement in local politics and advocacy groups can significantly improve your community. From shaping policies that impact education, health, and safety to protecting local parks and improving public services, your influence can lead to a legacy of betterment. It's a chance to plant trees under whose shade you may not sit but will provide respite for future generations. Your active participation ensures that your golden years are not just a time of reflection but of meaningful action that echoes beyond the confines of your immediate surroundings.

As we wrap up this exploration of civic engagement, remember that your voice is a powerful instrument, your experiences a unique lens, and your efforts a cornerstone of community resilience. Whether it's through running for office, joining advocacy groups, or leading campaigns, your engagement is a testament to the enduring spirit of active citizenship. As we turn the page from local involvement to exploring global connections in the next chapter, carry forward the understanding that your actions, big and small, weave into the larger tapestry of societal progress. Let's continue making waves from our backyards to the far reaches of our connected world.

One Last Thing...

I'm excited about all the possibilities ahead of you, and I hope you're ready to throw yourself into retirement with energy and enthusiasm. Before you do, though, take a moment to share this adventure with more people.

Simply by sharing your honest opinion of this book and a little about how it's helped you, you'll help new readers find it and shape their own retirement years with purpose.

TAKE A MOMENT TO SHARE YOUR THOUGHTS!

Thank you so much for your support. Enjoy every moment of the exciting new chapter ahead of you—you've earned it!

Scan the QR code below to leave your review.

CONCLUSION

As we conclude *Things to Do in Retirement That Unleash Play, Passion, and Purpose*, it's time to reflect on our incredible journey. The onset of retirement, a phase that might have initially seemed daunting, has now unfolded as a landscape filled with endless possibilities and vibrant opportunities. This book aims to guide you through the transition, offering a treasure trove of activities designed to reignite your passions, cultivate new interests, and foster a profound sense of purpose.

Throughout these pages, we've explored a magnitude of activities, each designed to inspire and motivate you to embrace this new chapter with enthusiasm. From the simple yet profoundly fulfilling joy of gardening to the dynamic world of digital adventures, we've covered a spectrum of pursuits that cater to diverse interests and abilities. The practical advice, uplifting stories from fellow retirees, and wealth of resources provided were all crafted to help evolve your retirement from a period of simple relaxation to a time of reinvention and joy.

We've underscored the essence of a fulfilling retirement by focusing on play, passion, and purpose. Play is about rediscovering the joys that bring a smile and sparkle to your eyes. Passion is about diving deep into activities that ignite your heart, making every day like a new adventure. Purpose is about finding meaningful ways to connect with others and contribute to your community, ensuring that your retirement is enjoyable and impactful.

We've also addressed the common concerns often accompanying this transition—identity shifts, health worries, and the fear of irrelevance. Through the shared experiences of those who have successfully navigated these challenges, we've seen that these concerns can be transformed into opportunities for growth and renewal.

The stories and experiences of real people showcased throughout this book are powerful reminders that retirement can be a time of vibrant living and continuous discovery. These narratives have demonstrated that regardless of your background, budget, or physical abilities, there are countless ways to make this stage of life extraordinarily rewarding.

As you move forward, please take advantage of the excitement and curiosity that have been the undercurrents of our journey together. Embrace the activities that resonate with you, and don't be afraid to try something new. Remember, this is your time to craft the retirement you've always dreamed of—a retirement that is uniquely yours, filled with play, passion, and purpose.

So, let's celebrate the beginning of this remarkable adventure. Your retirement is not just the end of a career but the start of an incredible new chapter. Dive into it with open arms, a curious mind, and a passionate heart. Here's to a retirement that is as dynamic, fulfilling, and extraordinary as you are. Enjoy every moment, and may your days be filled with joy, creativity, and profound purpose.

REFERENCES

10 solo senior travel tips. (2018, September 13). American Standard Walk-In Tubs. https://walkintubs.americanstandard-us.com/10-solo-senior-travel-tips/

3 kinds of exercise that boost heart health. (2021, November 3). Johns Hopkins Medicine. https://www.hopkinsmedicine.org/health/wellness-and-prevention/3-kinds-of-exercise-that-boost-heart-health

31 Inspiring Retirement Quotes to Get You Excited About A New Chapter. Sifton Properties. Last modified May 23, 2023. https://sifton.com/retirement-living/resident-resources/inspiring-retirement-quotes/

9 of the best volunteering opportunities for seniors. (2023, August 31). Whitestone. https://www.liveatwhitestone.org/news/best-volunteering-opportunities-for-seniors/

America's test kitchen online cooking school. (n.d.). America's Test Kitchen. https://www.onlinecookingschool.com/

AmeriCorps Seniors | AmeriCorps. (2020, November 9). AmeriCorps. https://americorps.gov/serve/americorps-seniors

AmeriCorps Seniors. (2020, November 9). AmeriCorps. https://americorps.gov/serve/americorps-seniors

Andrew, L. (2024, March 14). *7 unusual ways to cut your cost of living in retirement.* Yahoo Finance. https://finance.yahoo.com/news/7-unusual-ways-cut-cost-130042614.html

Basic Privacy Settings & Tools. (n.d.). Facebook. https://www.facebook.com/help/325807937506242

Beeson, J. (2018, July 11). *11 hiking tips for older adults.* Road Scholar. https://www.roadscholar.org/blog/11-hiking-tips-for-older-adults/

Benefits of social activities for seniors | Thorne Crest. (2018, May 24). *Thorne Crest Senior Living Community.* https://thornecrest.net/decision-guides-tools/the-benefits-of-social-activities-for-seniors/, https://thornecrest.net/decision-guides-tools/the-benefits-of-social-activities-for-seniors/

Bennett, R. L. (n.d.). *How to fund your retirement hobby.* Texas County & District Retirement System. https://www.tcdrs.org/library/how-to-fund-your-retirement-hobby/

Best places to sell your crafts online. (n.d.). The Design Trust. https://www.thedesigntrust.co.uk/best-places-to-sell-your-crafts-online/

Bethesda Senior Living. (n.d.). *A quick guide to starting a blog as a senior.* Autumn

View Gardens Assisted Living and Memory Care. https://www.autumnviewgardensellisville.com/blog/a-quick-guide-to-starting-a-blog-as-a-senior

Camping, cabins, RVs, permits, passes & more. (n.d.). Recreation.Gov. https://www.recreation.gov/

Chen, J. (2020a, November 30). *18 best online art classes for adults to try.* Teambuilding.com. https://teambuilding.com/blog/online-art-classes

Chen, J. (2020b, November 30). *18 best online art classes for adults to try.* Teambuilding.com. https://teambuilding.com/blog/online-art-classes

Choreograph Gainesville. (n.d.). *The joy of solo tours: Why seniors are embracing independent travel.* Choreograph Gainesville. https://choreographgainesville.com/blog/the-joy-of-solo-tours-why-seniors-are-embracing-independent-travel

Connie D. (2016, October 27). How to start your own craft club. *Sugar Bee Crafts.* https://sugarbeecrafts.com/start-craft-club

Cornell Lab of Ornithology. (n.d.). *Merlin bird ID by Cornell lab—Apps on Google Play.* https://play.google.com/store/apps/details?id=com.labs.merlinbirdid.app&hl=en_US

Corps Lakes Gateway Page. (n.d.). US Army Corps of Engineers. https://corpslakes.erdc.dren.mil/

DeMuro, K. (2013, July 11). *The many benefits of community gardens.* Greenleaf Communities. https://www.greenleafcommunities.org/the-many-benefits-of-community-gardens/

Doherty, P. (2023, August 16). *14 best senior-friendly travel groups.* Travel + Leisure. https://www.travelandleisure.com/trip-ideas/senior-travel/best-travel-groups-for-seniors

FSR. (2023, June 28). *9 tips for planning a community event.* First Service Residential. https://www.fsresidential.com/florida/news-events/articles/9-tips-for-successful-community-event-planning/

Glusac, E. (2022, September 22). Thrifty strategies for senior travelers. *The New York Times.* https://www.nytimes.com/2022/09/22/travel/frugal-strategies-for-senior-travelers.html

Guest Contributor. (2019, March 23). *A beginners guide to taking portraits of elderly clients: Part 2 – lighting and posing.* Digital Photography School. https://digital-photography-school.com/taking-portraits-of-elderly-clients-part-2-lighting-and-posing/

Hamingson, M. (n.d.). *How to market to senior citizens on social media.* Business News Daily. https://www.businessnewsdaily.com/10146-target-older-demographics-social-media.html

Hargreaves, A. (2019, July 11). 19 unique and totally awesome themed book club ideas. *BOOK RIOT.* https://bookriot.com/themed-book-club-ideas/

Hartman, R. (2021, November 3). *11 Seasonal Jobs for Retirees.* U.S. News. https://

money.usnews.com/money/retirement/second-careers/articles/seasonal-jobs-for-retirees

Hobby clubs activity ideas for seniors & the elderly. (n.d.). Golden Carers. https://www.goldencarers.com/hobby-clubs/

How to set retirement goals and where to start. (2023, October). Western & Southern Financial Group. https://www.westernsouthern.com/retirement/how-to-set-retirement-goals

Instrumentl Team. (2022, December 21). *Starting a charity: A 9-step beginner's guide.* Instrumentl. https://www.instrumentl.com/blog/how-to-start-charity

Leung, C., Wong, K. C., So, W. W. Y., Tse, Z. C. K., Li, D., Cao, Y., & Shum, D. H. K. (2022). The application of technology to improve cognition in older adults: A review and suggestions for future directions. *Psych Journal, 11*(4), 583–599. https://doi.org/10.1002/pchj.565

Leverette, M. M. (2024, February 10). *Growing vegetables in pots is easier than you think—Follow our beginner's guide.* The Spruce. https://www.thespruce.com/vegetable-container-gardening-for-beginners-848161

Long, J. (2021, September 2). Yoga for seniors: A sequence to help with your mobility. *Yoga Journal.* https://www.yogajournal.com/practice/yoga-sequences/yoga-for-seniors-sequence-to-help-with-mobility/

Loomis, S. (2022, May 2). How to start book clubs for seniors: Your guide. *BOOK RIOT.* https://bookriot.com/book-clubs-for-seniors/

Martinez, L., Gimenes, M., & Lambert, E. (2023). Video games and board games: Effects of playing practice on cognition. *PLOS ONE, 18*(3), e0283654. https://doi.org/10.1371/journal.pone.0283654

MasterClass. (2021, August 30). *How to Start Writing a Memoir: 10 Tips for Starting Your Memoir.* MasterClass. https://www.masterclass.com/articles/how-to-start-writing-a-memoir

McCormick, A., & Owens, H. (2024, January 31). *Best meditation apps of 2024.* Verywell Mind. https://www.verywellmind.com/best-meditation-apps-4767322

McGuiness, D. (2022, September 7). *The best documentaries for seniors on streaming services right now.* Oaks at Denville. https://oaksatdenville.org/news/best-documentaries-for-seniors-on-streaming-services/

Midyet, K. (2023, August 7). Thriving in retirement: Building resilience and positive mindsets. *Coaching Aging Adults.* https://www.coachingagingadults.com/thriving-in-retirement-building-resilience-and-positive-mindsets/

Munira, M. (2024, January 19). *Beginner's guide to choosing the best volunteer abroad project.* Volunteer Forever. https://www.volunteerforever.com/article_post/beginners-guide-to-choosing-the-best-volunteer-abroad-project/

Noyon, T. . A. (2024, April 29). *Freelancing after retirement: Tips for success.*

LinkedIn. https://www.linkedin.com/pulse/freelancing-after-retirement-tips-success-talha-ahmed-noyon-vvzsc

Online learning platforms for seniors. (2023, September 27). The Ormsby. https://www.ormsbyliving.org/about/news-blog/best-online-learning-platforms-for-older-adults/

Price, T. (2017, August 16). How to start a cookbook club. *BOOK RIOT.* https://bookriot.com/start-cookbook-club/

published, E. P. (2019, September 6). *The surprising benefits of gardening in retirement.* Personal Finance: Kiplinger. https://www.kiplinger.com/article/retirement/t013-c000-s004-the-surprising-benefits-of-gardening-in-retirement.html

Raghav, A. (n.d.). *Guide to social media for older adults.* Taking Care. https://taking.care/blogs/resources-advice/social-media-for-older-adults

Robinson, L., & Segal, J. (n.d.). *How to exercise with limited mobility.* HelpGuide.Org. https://www.helpguide.org/articles/healthy-living/chair-exercises-and-limited-mobility-fitness.htm

Robinson, L., & Smit , M. (n.d.). *Adjusting to retirement: Handling depression and stress.* HelpGuide.Org. https://www.helpguide.org/articles/aging-issues/adjusting-to-retirement.htm

Senior community gardening manual. (2022). Empowerline. https://www.empowerline.org/resource/senior-community-gardening-manual/

Shockley, M. M. (2022, December 25). 10 inspiring retirement stories you'll love from 2022. *TravelAwaits.* https://www.travelawaits.com/2843332/best-retirement-stories-2022/

Shuman, T. (n.d.). Senior discounts on cell phones in 2024. *SeniorLiving.Org.* https://www.seniorliving.org/finance/senior-discounts/

Start a walking group. (n.d.). AARP. https://createthegood.aarp.org/volunteer-guides/start-walking-group.html

Top 10 best podcasts for seniors. (n.d.). Senior Helpers. https://www.seniorhelpers.com/il/des-plaines/resources/blogs/top-10-best-podcasts-for-seniors/

Top 5 best apps for seniors and the elderly of 2024. (2023, April 29). Speechify. https://speechify.com/blog/best-apps-for-seniors-and-the-elderly/

Valentine, R. (2023, October 2). *How a guild of 'old timers' is embracing online gaming all the way to retirement.* IGN. https://www.ign.com/articles/how-a-guild-of-old-timers-is-embracing-online-gaming-all-the-way-to-retirement

Volunteer match—Where volunteering begins. (n.d.). Volunteer Match. https://www.volunteermatch.org/

Weinger, A. (2022, April 6). Nonprofit basics: Museum membership. *Double the Donation.* https://doublethedonation.com/museum-membership/

Weitzman. (2023, April 29). *Top 5 best apps for seniors and the elderly of 2024.* Speechify. https://speechify.com/blog/best-apps-for-seniors-and-the-elderly/

Winter, D. (2024, March 22). *Turning a hobby into a business in 9 easy steps(2024).* Shopify. https://www.shopify.com/blog/hobby-to-business

Wolfson, J., & Leung, C. (2020, June 2). *The joy of cooking and its benefits for older adults.* National Poll on Healthy Aging. https://www.healthyagingpoll.org/reports-more/report/joy-cooking-and-its-benefits-older-adults

Made in United States
Troutdale, OR
12/04/2024